Great Funny Quotes

Great Funny Quotes

Sweeten Your Life with Laughter

DAVID YOUNG

Wind Runner Press
Round Rock, Texas

Great funny quotes : sweeten your life with laughter / [compiled by] David Young. –1st ed.
ISBN-13: 978-1-936179-01-5
ISBN-10: 1-936179-01-6
Library of Congress Control Number: 2011944534

Introduction

"We don't laugh because we're happy – we're happy because we laugh," according to philosopher and psychologist William James. *Great Funny Quotes* gives you 2,335 reasons to laugh and be happy. Stressed at work? Burnt out from taking care of the kids? Overwhelmed by family, financial or health problems? Regardless of your situation, this hilarious book will give you an instant vacation, a chance to relax, renew your spirit and gain a fresh perspective – so vital to overcoming life's toughest challenges. Or maybe you've lost your joy. If so, this book can help you too. As Josh Billings said, "Laughter is the fireworks of the soul." So relax and enjoy *Great Funny Quotes,* and sweeten your life with laughter.

Accidents

The Lord Chief Justice of England recently said that the greatest part of his judicial time was spent investigating collisions between propelled vehicles, each on its own side of the road, each sounding its horn and each stationary.

— *Philip Guedalla*

Accordions

Accordion: A bagpipe with pleats.

— *Anonymous*

Accountants

An accountant is someone who solves a problem you didn't know you had in a way you don't understand.

— *Anonymous*

The old accountant retired after fifty years, and in the top drawer of his desk they found a note that said: "Debits in the column toward the file cabinet. Credits in the column toward the window."

— *Anonymous*

I once had an accountant who was so good with numbers he eventually got to wear one for ten to fifteen years.

— *Gene Perret*

Actions

Actions speak louder than words – but not so often.

— *Anonymous*

Actors

An actor's success has the life expectancy of a small boy about to look into a gas tank with a lighted match.

— *Fred Allen*

Acting is pretending, and the most difficult part is pretending you're eating regularly.

— *Anonymous*

There are five stages in the life of an actor: Who's Mary Astor? Get me Mary Astor. Get me a Mary Astor type. Get me a young Mary Astor. Who's Mary Astor?

— Mary Astor

She goes, "I'm an actress." I go, "Sure, which restaurant?"

— Sarah Bernhard

The most important thing in acting is honesty. If you can fake that, you've got it made.

— George Burns

My career must be slipping. This is the first time I've been available to pick up an award.

— Michael Caine

The last time I acted my name was so low on the program that I was getting orders for the printing.

— Frank Carson

I had one guy at a gas station in New York say to me, "Hey, you look like that Hugh Grant. No offense."

— Hugh Grant

The only great acting we see nowadays is from the losing nominees on Oscar Night.

— Will Rogers

Admiration
Admiration: Our polite recognition of another's resemblance to ourselves.
— Ambrose Bierce

Adolescence
Adolescence is the time in life when a youngster is well informed about anything he doesn't have to study.

— Anonymous

Adolescence begins when children stop asking questions – because they know all the answers.

— *Evan Esar*

Adolescence is that period in a kid's life when parents become more difficult.

— *Ryan O'Neal*

Adolescence is perhaps nature's way of preparing parents to welcome the empty nest.

— *Karen Savage and Patricia Adams*

A normal adolescent isn't a normal adolescent if he acts normal.

— *Judith Viorst*

Adults
Adult: A person who has stopped growing at both ends and started growing in the middle.

— *Anonymous*

Advancement
Yesterday I was a dog. Today I'm a dog. Tomorrow I'll probably still be a dog. Sigh! There's so little hope for advancement.

— *Snoopy*

Adversity
Never position a rock near a hard place.

— *Rohan Candappa*

I understand life isn't fair, but why couldn't it just once be unfair in my favor?

— *Christy Murphy*

We all have strength enough to endure the misfortune of others.

— *François de La Rochefoucauld*

There are those who imagine that the unlucky accidents of life – life's experiences – are in some way useful to us. I wish I could find out how. I never knew one of them to happen twice.

— *Mark Twain*

Advertisements

Whenever you hear the word *save,* it is usually the beginning of an advertisement designed to make you spend money.

— *Anonymous*

Advice

We hate to have some people give us advice because we know how badly they need it themselves.

— *Anonymous*

Among the many remedies that won't cure a cold, the most common is advice.

— *Anonymous*

The best time to give advice to your children is while they're still young enough to believe you know what you're talking about.

— *Anonymous*

Don't be discouraged if your children reject your advice. Years later they will offer it to their offspring.

— *Anonymous*

When a man comes to me for advice, I find out the kind of advice he wants, and give it to him.

— *Josh Billings*

When your mother asks, "Do you want a piece of advice?" it's a mere formality. It doesn't matter if you answer yes or no. You're going to get it anyway.

— *Erma Bombeck*

Whenever a man seeks your advice he generally seeks your praise.

— *Lord Chesterfield*

We always admire the intelligence of those who ask us for advice.

— *Ramsey Clark*

No vice is so bad as advice.

— *Marie Dressler*

When we ask advice we are usually looking for an accomplice.

— *Charles de La Grange*

I intended to give you some advice but now I remember how much is left over from last year unused.

— *George Harris*

If you want to get rid of somebody, just tell him something for his own good.

— *Kin Hubbard*

The trouble with giving advice is that people want to repay you.

— *Franklin Jones*

Advice is what we ask for when we already know the answer but wish we didn't.

— *Erica Jong*

You will always find some Eskimo ready to instruct the Congolese on how to cope with heatwaves.

— *Stanislaw Lec*

Like so many contemporary philosophers, he especially enjoyed giving helpful advice to people who were happier than he was.

— *Tom Lehrer*

For sincere advice and the correct time, call any number at random at 3:00 a.m.

— *Steve Martin*

The one prediction that never comes true is, "You'll thank me for telling you this."

— *Judith Martin "Miss Manners"*

Many years ago a wise man took me aside. "Harpo, my boy," he said, "I'm going to give you three pieces of advice, three things you should always remember." My heart jumped and I glowed with excitement. I was going to hear the magic password to a rich, full life from the master himself. "Yes, sir." I said. And he told me the three things. I regret I've forgotten what they were.

— *Harpo Marx*

I give myself sometimes admirable advice, but I am incapable of taking it.
— *Lady Mary Montagu*

No matter what, Dad was always there with solid words of advice . . . "Go ask your mother."

— *Alan Ray*

If you want people to notice your faults, start giving advice.
— *Kelly Stephens*

I always advise people never to give advice.

— *P.G. Wodehouse*

Aerobics
Eternity is the second ten minutes of aerobics.

— *Anonymous*

The word aerobics comes from two Greek words: *aero,* meaning "ability to," and *bics,* meaning "withstand tremendous boredom."

— *Dave Barry*

The word aerobics came about when the gym instructors got together and said, "If we're going to charge ten dollars an hour, we can't call it Jumping Up and Down."

— *Rita Rudner*

Age
Warning: Dates on calendar are closer than they appear.

— *Anonymous*

It's hard to know just where one generation ends and the next one begins, but it's somewhere around 9:00 p.m.

— Anonymous

Aging: Eventually you will reach a point when you stop lying about your age and start bragging about it.

— Anonymous

Memory expert: A woman who has once been told another woman's right age.

— Anonymous

You leave concerts and ball games early to beat the crowd.

— Anonymous, You're not a kid anymore when . . .

A clever wife doesn't lie about her age: she just says she's as old as her husband, and then lies about his age.

— Anonymous

The best way to cure your wife of anything is to tell her it's caused by advancing age.

— Anonymous

When you are dissatisfied and would like to go back to your youth, think of algebra.

— Anonymous

Time may be a great healer, but it's a lousy beautician.

— Anonymous

When we're young, we want to change the world. When we're old, we want to change the young.

— Anonymous

People call you at 8:00 p.m. and ask: "Did I wake you?"

— Anonymous, You're not a kid anymore when . . .

I'm only fourteen.
— *Nadia Comaneci, when asked after winning the gold medal if she was going to retire*

Wrinkles are hereditary. Parents get them from their children.
— *Doris Day*

The years that a woman subtracts from her age are not lost. They are added to the ages of other women.
— *Diane de Poitiers*

The older you get, you're just too tired to care about the same things. Rock concerts, I used to camp out for tickets. Now you could tell me Barbara Streisand is playing for free down the street, and I'd say, "How far down the street? Let's just stay here and watch the Discovery Channel. C'mon, it's Shark Week!"
— *Kathleen Madigan*

A woman telling her true age is like a buyer confiding his final price to an Armenian rug dealer.
— *Mignon McLaughlin*

If you're less than ten years old you're so excited about aging you think in fractions. "How old are you?" "Six and a half!" You're never 36 and a half. Then a strange thing happens. If you make it over 100 you become a kid again. "I'm 104. And a half!"
— *Larry Miller*

Ask any woman her age, and nine times out of ten she'll guess wrong.
— *Bob Murphy*

You're seriously concerned when you're a kid that you might not be able to take the excitement of being an adult, of driving around and people calling on the phone and getting mail addressed directly to you. Now, it's like: "You drive; tell 'em I'm not here; and I can't believe all this junk mail!"
— *Jerry Seinfeld*

There are only two things a child will share willingly – communicable diseases and his mother's age.

— Dr. Benjamin Spock

As long as a woman can look ten years younger than her own daughter she is perfectly satisfied.

— Oscar Wilde

The old believe everything, the middle-aged suspect everything, and the young know everything.

— Oscar Wilde

It's hard to keep up with the younger people coming up.

— Kim Zmeskal, sixteen-year-old gymnast

Age, Middle

Middle age: When a woman's hair starts turning from gray to black.

— Anonymous

I would feel a lot more middle-aged if I knew more ninety-year-olds.

— Anonymous, on turning 45

Don't worry about middle age; you'll outgrow it.

— Anonymous

Did you ever notice: The Roman Numerals for forty are XL.

— Anonymous

One of the chief pleasures of middle age is looking back at the people you didn't marry.

— Anonymous

Middle age is when your classmates are so gray and wrinkled and bald they don't recognize you.

— Bennett Cerf

Just after my thirtieth birthday, instead of growing hair on my head, I now was growing it in places where I didn't need it, like the top of my ear.

A strand had sprouted there overnight and made me look like something out of *The Cat in the Hat*.

— *Bill Cosby*

I recently turned fifty, which is young for a tree, midlife for an elephant, and ancient for a quarter-miler, whose son now says, "Dad, I just can't run the quarter with you anymore unless I bring something to read."

— *Bill Cosby*

Middle age is when your broad mind and narrow waist begin to change places.

— *E. Joseph Cossman*

Ladies don't have a Senior Tour. They won't admit when they turn fifty.

— *Deisy Flood*

You know you're fifty if it takes three tries to call your kids by correct names.

— *Bill Geist*

At a cheerful lunch with old friends, questions arise: "When was that, that we went to that great place, you know the place, with those guys, you know who I mean, what's his name and what's her face? Oh, where was that? I can't remember why on earth we went there, but it was fun. Wasn't it?"

— *Bill Geist, on turning fifty*

A woman can tell she's fifty if she can periodically defrost a Hungry-Man Double Entrée TV dinner with her bare hands.

— *Bill Geist*

Middle age is when your age starts to show around your middle.

— *Bob Hope*

I have everything now I had twenty years ago, except now it's all lower.

— *Gypse Rose Lee*

Middle age is when you stop criticizing the older generation and start criticizing the younger one.

— *Laurence Peter*

When you are about 35 years old, something terrible always happens to music.

— *Steve Race*

I can define middle-aged. That's when you're faced with two temptations and you choose the one that'll get you home at nine o'clock.

— *Ronald Reagan*

Age, Old

Remember when we used to laugh at old people when we were young? Do you recall what was so funny?

— *Anonymous*

Seen it all, done it all, can't remember most of it.

— *Anonymous*

To me old age is always fifteen years older than I am.

— *Bernard Baruch*

If I'd known I was gonna live this long, I'd have taken better care of myself.

— *Eubie Blake, on his hundredth birthday*

What's nice about the Senior Tour is you can't remember your bad shots.

— *Bob Bruce*

By the time you're eighty years old you've learned everything. You only have to remember it.

— *George Burns*

I was brought up to respect my elders and now I don't have to respect anybody.

— *George Burns, at age 87*

You know you're getting old when you stoop to tie your shoes and wonder what else you can do while you're down there.

— *George Burns*

I was introduced to a beautiful young lady as a man in his nineties. Early nineties, I insisted.

— *George Burns*

Don't worry about senility – when it hits you, you won't know it.

— *Bill Cosby*

I don't know how you feel about old age, but in my case I didn't even see it coming. It hit me from the rear.

— *Phyllis Diller*

I'm at the age when my back goes out more than I do.

— *Phyllis Diller*

Eighty is a wonderful age – especially if you're ninety.

— *Abel Green*

An elderly woman in a nursing home declined her pastor's suggestion that she get a hearing aid. "At 91, I've heard enough," she said.

— *Catherine Hall*

In youth we want to change the world. In old age we want to change youth.

— *Garth Henrichs*

Oh to be seventy again.
— *Oliver Wendell Holmes, Jr., on seeing an attractive woman on his ninetieth birthday*

Forty is the old age of youth; fifty is the youth of old age.

— *Victor Hugo*

Children are a great comfort in your old age – and they help you reach it faster too.

— *Richard Kauffmann*

"Oh to be old again," said a young corpse.

— *Stanislaw Lec*

You know you're getting old when you start watching golf on TV and enjoy it.

— *Larry Miller*

I'm now old enough to personally identify every object in antique stores.

— *Anita Milner*

I'm at the age where I have to find my hearing aid to ask where my glasses are.

— *Robert Orben*

You know you're getting old when all the names in your black book have M.D. after them.

— *Arnold Palmer*

Old age is when you know all the answers, but nobody asks you the questions.

— *Laurence Peter*

People tell me, "Gee, you look good." There are three ages of man: youth, middle age and "Gee, you look good."

— *Red Skelton*

When you get old, everything is hurting. When I get up in the morning, it sounds like I'm making popcorn.

— *Lawrence Taylor*

I knew I was getting old when the Pope started looking young.

— *Billy Wilder*

Alarm Clocks
Alarm clock: An instrument used to wake up people who have no kids.

— *Anonymous*

Alaska
In Alaska, we have just two seasons – this winter and next winter.

— *Leigh Wade*

Alliances

Alliance: In international politics, the union of two thieves who have their hands so deeply inserted in each other's pocket that they cannot separately plunder a third.

— *Ambrose Bierce*

Allowances

One of the first things a child learns at school is that some other child is getting a bigger allowance.

— *Anonymous*

Another thing a small boy is constantly outgrowing is his allowance.

— *Anonymous*

Anger

Angry wife to husband: "You are being deliberately calm."

— *Anonymous*

I don't enjoy playing video golf because there's nothing to throw.

— *Paul Azinger*

I was always more of a breaker than a thrower – mostly putters. I broke so many of those, I probably became the world's foremost authority on how to putt without a putter.

— *Tommy Bolt*

Righteous indignation: Your own wrath as opposed to the shocking bad temper of others.

— *Elbert Hubbard*

The most exquisitely satisfying act in the world of golf is that of throwing a club. The full backswing, the delayed wrist action, the flowing follow-through, followed by that unique whirring sound, reminiscent only of a passing flock of starlings, are without parallel in sport.

— *Henry Longhurst*

You missed your calling. You should have been an usher.
   — *Sandy Mayer, to John McEnroe after he told a fan to shut up and sit down*

Why am I using a new putter? Because the old one didn't float too well.

— *Craig Stadler*

Anniversaries

Wedding anniversary: Easy for a golfer to remember. "How could I forget? It's June fifteenth – on that day in 1953 I missed a two-inch putt on the fifteenthth hole."

— *Martin Ragaway*

Antiques

Antique: An object which has made a round trip to the attic.

— *Anonymous*

Antique: Something nobody liked well enough to wear it out.

— *Anonymous*

If you don't know what you want, we have it.

— *Sign in antique shop*

If something's old and you're trying to sell it, it's obsolete; if you're trying to buy it, it's a collector's item.

— *Frank Ross*

Apologies

It takes real talent to be able to apologize in a manner that makes the offended person feel guilty.

— *Anonymous*

Appearance

I refuse to think of them as chin hairs. I think of them as stray eyebrows.

— *Janette Barber*

If you're a man, at some point a woman will ask you how she looks. "How do I look?" she'll ask. You must be careful how you answer this question. The best technique is to form an honest yet sensitive opinion, then collapse on the floor with some kind of fatal seizure. Trust me, this is the easiest way out. Because you will never come up with the right answer.

— *Dave Barry*

Thanks. You don't look so hot yourself.
— *Yogi Berra, to Mayor John Lindsay's wife after she said he looked cool in his suit*

Did you ever look in a mirror and wonder how your pantyhose got so wrinkled . . . and then remember you weren't wearing any?
— *Phyllis Diller*

She takes herself asunder still when she goes to bed, into some twenty boxes; and about next day noon is put together again, like a great German clock.
— *Ben Jonson*

I don't know who would want to win it. I sure wouldn't want to win it.
— *Joe Paterno, on a Joe Paterno look-alike contest staged by the student body*

My girlfriend has lovely colored eyes. I particularly like the blue one.
— *Harry Scott*

The difference between Namath and me is that when you make the money he makes, they say you're ruggedly handsome. When you make the money I make, they say you have a big nose.
— *Jim Valvano, on being told he looked like Joe Namath*

Appetizers
Appetizers are little things you keep eating until you lose your appetite.
— *Richard Armour*

Approval
At twenty, we don't care what the world thinks of us; at thirty, we worry about what it's thinking of us; at forty, we discover it isn't thinking about us at all.
— *Anonymous*

Arguments
There are two sides to every argument, and they're usually married to each other.
— *Anonymous*

The only people who listen to both sides of a family quarrel are the next-door neighbors.

— *Anonymous*

There are two theories of arguing with women. Neither one works.

— *Anonymous*

My wife was too beautiful for words, but not for arguments.

— *John Barrymore*

Children are intensely invested in getting their way. They will devote more emotional and intellectual energy to winning arguments than parents ever will, and are almost always better rested.

— *Jean Callahan*

I've never won an argument with her; and the only times I thought I had I found out the argument wasn't over yet.

— *Jimmy Carter, on wife Rosalynn*

It is astonishing how articulate one can become when alone and raving at a radio. Arguments and counter arguments, rhetoric and bombast flow from one's lips like scurf from the hair of a bank manager.

— *Stephen Fry*

My wife and I had words – but I never got to use mine.

— *Carl Gilligan*

I got into an argument with my girlfriend inside a tent. A tent is not a good place for an argument. I tried to walk out on her and had to slam the flap.

— *Mitch Hedberg*

No matter what side of an argument you're on, you always find some people on your side that you wish were on the other side.

— *Jascha Heifetz*

Art
The painting [Whistler's Mother] shows this nice old lady who is waiting for the repairman to bring back her TV set.

— *Anonymous, kindergartner*

Can't you paint on walls like other children? Do you have any idea how hard it is to get that stuff off the ceiling?

— *Michelangelo's mother*

Rembrandt painted 700 pictures. Of these 3,000 are in existence.

— *Wilhelm Bode*

Abstract art is a product of the untalented sold by the unprincipled to the utterly bewildered.

— *Al Capp*

The murals in restaurants are about on a par with the food in art galleries.

— *Peter DeVries*

Whatever else you do, sign it. If you do that, we will know which way to hold it.

— *Auguste Rodin, to Picasso regarding his latest painting*

Attics
An attic is a place where you keep something for ten years and then throw it away two weeks before you need it.

— *Anonymous*

Auctions
Never wave to a friend at an auction.

— *Anonymous*

Authority
In an office the authority of a person is inversely proportional to the number of pens they are carrying.

— *Anonymous*

Auto Racing
Auto racing is boring except when a car is going at least 172 mph upside-down.

— *Dave Barry*

Driving a race car is like dancing with a chainsaw.

— *Cale Yarborough*

Autographs

I went to the men's room and I was standing there at the urinal and I get a tap on the shoulder and this guy's standing there with a placemat and a pen asking me for my autograph. He said he didn't want to bother me while I was having lunch.

— Vince Lombardi

Every time I sign a ball, and there have been thousands, I thank my luck that I wasn't born Coveleski, or Wambsganss or Peckinpaugh.

— Mel Ott

Signing autographs was fun until a kid came up to me and said, "My dad says you're getting old, you're going to die and your autograph will be valuable."

— Warren Spahn

Autumn

Autumn is the most beautiful time of the year to the person who has no leaves to rake.

— Anonymous

Babies

Sterilize: What you do to your baby's first pacifier by boiling it, and to your last baby's pacifier by blowing on it and wiping it with saliva.

— Anonymous

Out of the mouth of babes come things parents never should have said.

— Anonymous

Fill a small bag with twelve pounds of wet sand. At 8:00 p.m., begin to waltz and hum with the bag until 9:00 p.m. Lie down and get up again immediately. Sing every song you have ever heard. Fall asleep standing up, then make breakfast. Do this for five years. Look cheerful. Congratulations, you have now passed the baby night test.

— Anonymous

Two-minute warning: When your baby's face turns red and she begins to make those familiar grunting noises.

— Anonymous

How come the second baby isn't as breakable as the first?

> — *Anonymous*

If you want to know what it's like to feed a baby, sit at the kitchen counter and carefully spoon strained peas and chocolate pudding into a plastic bag. When the bag is completely full, tie a knot to close it, place it on the kitchen counter at eye level about a foot from your face, then ask your spouse to smash the bag with a dictionary.

> — *Anonymous*

Out of the mouths of babes comes cereal.

> — *Anonymous*

Most people make babies out to be very complicated, but the truth is they have only three moods:
>   Mood one: Just about to cry.
>   Mood two: Crying.
>   Mood three: Just finished crying.

> — *Dave Barry*

Babies do not take solid food through their mouths, which are generally occupied with other objects. Babies absorb solid food through their chins. You can save yourself a lot of frustrating effort if you smear the food directly on your baby's chin, rather than putting it in the baby's mouth and forcing the baby to expel it on to its chin, as many uninformed parents do.

> — *Dave Barry*

In a typical magazine ad for an educational toy, a baby is looking thoughtfully (for a baby) at two pieces of plastic. According to the ad, the pieces of plastic are helping the baby *acquire skills of problem solving.* In fact, the only problem the baby is solving is the problem of how to get both pieces in his mouth.

> — *Dave Barry*

Taking care of a newborn baby means devoting yourself, body and soul, 24 hours a day, seven days a week, to the welfare of someone whose major response, in the way of positive reinforcement, is to throw up on you.

> — *Dave Barry*

Great Funny Quotes

If you were to open up a baby – and I am not for a minute suggesting that you should – you would find that 85 to 90 percent of the space reserved for bodily organs is taken up by huge, highly active drool glands.

— *Dave Barry*

There are two distinct phases in the baby's language development. The second phase is when the baby actually starts talking, which is at about eighteen months. The first phase is when the parents imagine that the baby is talking, which is somewhere around twelve months, or even earlier if it's their first baby.

— *Dave Barry*

Out of the mouth of babes – usually when you've got your best suit on.

— *Geraldine Baxter*

Dressing a baby is like putting an octopus into a string bag, making sure none of the arms hang out.

— *Chris Evans*

A man finds out what is meant by a spitting image when he tries to feed cereal to his infant.

— *Imogene Fey*

Did you know babies are nauseated by the smell of a clean shirt?

— *Jeff Foxworthy*

Families with babies and families without babies are sorry for each other.

— *Edgar Howe*

Home alone with a wakeful newborn, I could shower so quickly that the mirror didn't fog and the backs of my knees stayed dry.

— *Marni Jackson*

Whatever is on the floor will wind up in your baby's mouth. Whatever is in your baby's mouth will wind up on the floor.

— *Bruce Lansky*

When your first baby drops its doll, you sterilize it. When your second baby drops its doll, you tell the dog to "Fetch!"

— *Bruce Lansky*

No baby is admired sufficiently to please the parents.

— *E.V. Lucas*

Shouldn't there be some kind of relationship between how much a baby eats and what comes out the other end? It's like that tiny clown car at the circus and all the clowns keep coming out and out and out.

— *Dennis Miller*

The first thing I thought when I saw my son was, "I wonder if they'd look less like space aliens if I penciled in their eyebrows."

— *Judith Newman*

A baby is an angel whose wings decrease as his legs increase.

— *French proverb*

The baby wakes up in the wee wee hours of the morning.

— *Robert Robbins*

Giving away baby clothes and nursery furniture is a major cause of pregnancy.

— *Esther Selsdon*

My friend's baby had an accident in its diaper. The mother comes over and says, "Oh, how adorable. Brandon made a gift for Daddy." I'm thinking this guy must be real easy to shop for on Father's Day.

— *Gary Shandling*

We learn from experience. A woman never wakes up her second baby just to see it smile.

— *Grace Williams*

Babies come with pint-sized tanks; they need fill-ups as often as any guzzler. So whenever you have a spare moment to sit, you automatically will know it's time to get up and feed your baby.

— *Teryl Zarnow*

Babysitters

Babysitter: A teenager you pay $7 an hour to eat $20 worth of snacks.

— Anonymous

When you're young, your mother tells you what time you have to be home; when you're grown up and married, your babysitter tells you.

— Anonymous

The modern couple usually gets along fine with their mother-in-law because they can't afford another babysitter.

— Anonymous

It's a good thing to have children while your parents are still young enough to take care of them.

— Rita Rudner

Grandmas are great babysitters, and they're less likely to sneak boys over.

— Dee Ann Stewart

Bachelors

Bachelor: A man who has faults he doesn't know about.

— Anonymous

Bad Luck

The first pull on the cord will send the drapes the wrong way.

— Anonymous

A falling nozzle will turn toward you and land on its trigger.

— Anonymous

Misfortune: The kind of fortune that never misses.

— Ambrose Bierce

When ripping an article from the newspaper, the tear is always into and never away from the required article.

— Alan Fraser

Losing one glove is sorrow enough, but nothing compared with the pain of losing one glove, discarding the other, then finding the first one again.

— *Piet Hein*

Buttered bread always falls dry side up.

— *Jewish proverb*

Bagels

Bagel: A doughnut dipped in cement.

— *Anonymous*

Bagpipes

What's the difference between a bagpipe and an onion? Nobody cries when you chop up a bagpipe.

— *Anonymous*

A true gentleman is a man who knows how to play the bagpipes – but doesn't.

— *Anonymous*

The bagpipes sound exactly the same when you have finished learning them as when you start.

— *Thomas Beecham*

The inventor of the bagpipes was inspired when he saw a man carrying an indignant asthmatic pig under his arm.

— *Alfred Hitchcock*

Baldness

Little boy to grandfather: "Are you still growing, Granddad?"

Grandfather: "I don't think so. Why do you ask?"

Boy: "It's just that the top of your head's coming out through your hair."

— *Anonymous*

I want my hair cut like my daddy's – with a hole on top.

— *Anonymous*

The most delightful advantage of being bald – one can hear snowflakes.

— *R.G. Daniels*

There's one thing about baldness – it's neat.

— *Don Herold*

Bald men. They get older and gravity starts sucking their hair back into their scalp, and shooting it out their ears.

— *Maryellen Hooper*

Life is a series of unfulfilled dreams. For instance, I always wanted to wear my hair long. At least, a lot longer than I did.

— *Robert Orben*

My son has a new nickname for me. He calls me "Baldy." Son, I have a new word for you, "Heredity."

— *Don Savage*

I don't consider myself bald. I'm simply taller than my hair.

— *Tom Sharp*

Barbers don't charge him for cutting his hair. They charge him for searching for it.

— *Henny Youngman*

Banks

Ever notice that we trust banks with our money, but they don't trust us with their pens?

— *Anonymous*

A bank is a place where they lend you an umbrella in fair weather and ask for it back again when it begins to rain.

— *Robert Frost*

Some banks require that you leave two signature cards – one for how your signature looks normally, and one for how it looks when the chain on their pen isn't long enough.

— *Gene Perret*

One bank recently went through a major reorganization. They discovered they had more vice presidents than depositors.

— *Gene Perret*

Banks will lend you money if you can prove you don't need it.

— *Mark Twain*

Barbecue

How is it that one careless match can start a forest fire, but it takes a whole box to start a barbecue?

— *Anonymous*

Barbecue: Smoke without fire.

— *Colin Bowles*

Men like to barbecue. Men like to cook only if danger is involved.

— *Rita Rudner*

Barbers

Just give me a shave. I haven't got time to listen to a haircut.

— *Anonymous*

I want little conversation and lots of hair on the floor.

— *Bum Phillips, on what he expects from a barber*

Bargains

A bargain is something you have to find a use for after you buy it.

— *Benjamin Franklin*

One of the most difficult tasks in the world is to convince a woman that even a bargain costs money.

— *Edgar Howe*

A bargain is something you can't use at a price you can't resist.

— *Franklin Jones*

Baseball

Just give me 25 guys on the last year of their contract; I'll win a pennant every year.

— *Sparky Anderson*

If you want to see a baseball game in the worst way – take your wife along.

— *Anonymous*

I don't see how either team can possibly win.

— *Anonymous*

You know you're getting bad when your wife takes you aside and tries to change your batting stance. And you take her advice.

— *Thomas Boswell*

If a tie is like kissing your sister, losing is like kissing your grandmother with her teeth out.

— *George Brett*

The announcer said, "Will the lady who lost her nine children at the ballpark please pick them up immediately. They are beating the Cubs, 10-0, in the seventh."

— *Tom Dressen*

A baseball game is twice as much fun if you're seeing it on the company's time.

— *William Feather*

A critic once characterized baseball as six minutes of action crammed into two-and-one-half hours.

— *Ray Fitzgerald*

I tell him, "Attaway to hit, George."
— *Jim Frey, as Royals manager, on what advice he gave to George Brett about hitting*

Knowing all about baseball is just about as profitable as being a good whittler.

— *Kin Hubbard*

Baseball is like watching grass – no, Astroturf, grow.

— *Jeff Jarvis*

When I first became a manager, I asked Chuck Tanner for advice. He told me, "Always rent."

— *Tony LaRussa*

All I know is that the way we're hitting, sick people are getting out of bed and wanting to pitch against us.

— *Bob Lemon*

Take your daughter to work day is coming up soon, April 26. Finally, a chance for the Detroit Tigers to win a game.

— *Jay Leno*

I'm going to Radio Shack to buy one of those headsets like the broadcasters use. It seems as soon as you put them on, you get 100 times smarter.

— *Nick Leyva, Phillies manager, on being tired of criticism from the TV booth*

Your Holiness, I'm Joseph Medwick. I, too, used to be a Cardinal.

— *Ducky Medwick*

When somebody on your team hits the wall making a catch, you say, "What guts. What a gamer." When a guy on the other team does it, you say, "What a dummy. There's no percentage in that."

— *Ray Miller*

There are days when you know that God invented baseball to give us all a concept of eternity.

— *Michael Olesker*

Whenever *whom* is required, recast the sentence. This keeps a huge section of the hard disk of your mind available for baseball averages.

— *William Safire*

Baseball is something of a ballet; the trouble is that the music is substandard – they use pretty much the same score at the hockey rink – and the performers often spit tobacco juice all over the place.

— *Dave Shiflett*

The thing is, a lot of the people who make these suggestions would have a hard time filling out the application forms to work at 7-Eleven.

— *Andy Van Slyke, on advice he received during a slump*

The most important thing our little league had was equipment. We were so tickled with our uniforms that we would show up for a 6:30 twilight game at noon.

— *Bob Turley*

For the parent of a Little Leaguer, a baseball game is simply a nervous breakdown divided into innings.

— *Earl Wilson*

I've been doing my best not to think about it, but by trying so hard not to think about it, I can't stop thinking about it.

— *Paul Zuvella, during an 0-for-28 slump*

Basketball

Old basketball players never die. They just sit in front of you at the movies.

— *Anonymous*

It was so bad, my travel agent called me with a play – and I wrote it down.

— *Benny Dees, on a slump during his days as coach of Wyoming*

I guess I must have rated between two and five.

— *Mike Fratello, on Atlanta management calling him one of the five best coaches in the NBA shortly before firing him*

That usually means you can't shoot.

— *Hosie Grimsley, on being named one of the top five defenders in college basketball by Dick Vitale*

I call Los Angeles the city of alternatives. If you don't like mountains, we got the ocean. If you don't like Knott's Berry Farm, we've got Disneyland. If you don't like basketball, we've got the Clippers.

— *Arsenio Hall*

Things got so bad that I had to play my student manager for a while. Things got really bad when she started to complain to the press that she wasn't getting enough playing time.

— *Linda Hill-McDonald*

The more Final Fours you go to, the more cousins you find you have who need tickets.

— *Mike Krzyzewski*

Don't bother. Somebody already swiped the sports section.

— *Mark Landsberger, after a teammate picked up the* Wall Street Journal

The phone rang and my wife told me it was *Sports Illustrated.* I cut myself shaving and fell down the steps in my rush to get to the phone. I said hello and a voice on the other end said, "For just 75 cents an issue . . ."

— *Speedy Morris*

Bobby Knight is a good friend of mine. But if I ever need a heart transplant, I want his. It's never been used.

— *George Raveling*

Whenever you lose, there's going to be criticism. That's why they invented talk radio.

— *Rudy Tomjanovich*

Bathrooms
Guest towel: A small square of non-absorbent fabric surrounded by water-proof embroidery.

— *Anonymous*

We were all great singers in our house. We had to be.
Why?
There was no lock on the bathroom door.

— Anonymous

How did I learn to dance? Simple – when I grew up there were six kids and only one bathroom.

— Anonymous

How long a minute is, depends on which side of the bathroom door you are on.

— Anonymous

A bathroom is a place where your child doesn't need to go until you're backing your car out of the driveway.

— Anonymous

However much a shower control may rotate, the degree of rotation required to change from ice-cold to scalding is never more than one millimeter.

— Joe Bennett

There is a special bathroom in heaven for the father of girls.

— Tommy Birch

When a child is locked in the bathroom with water running and says he's doing nothing, but the dog is barking, call 911.

— Erma Bombeck

Check for toilet paper *before* sitting down.

— H. Jackson Brown, Jr.

Bath Mat: A little rug that wet children like to stand next to.

— Ron Dentinger

Bath time is successful when your kids get wetter than you do.

— Dee Ann Stewart

Beans

A bean supper will be held Saturday evening in the church basement. Music will follow.

— Church bulletin

Beauty

Beauty always comes from within – within jars, tubes and compacts.

— Anonymous

Better that a girl has beauty than brains because boys see better than they think.

— Anonymous

If a man hears much that a woman says, she is not beautiful.

— Henry Haskins

She got her good looks from her father – he's a plastic surgeon.

— Groucho Marx

Bibles

I jjjust aaasked eeeach ppprospect if he wwwanted to bbbuy a Bbbible, or hhhave me rrread it to hhhim.

— Jim Reed, on how he sold more Bibles than anyone else

Bicycles

No matter which direction you go, it's uphill and against the wind.

— Laurence Peter, Peter's Bicycling Law

Big

In order to resemble William Perry, we have rented a Winnebago for our offensive line to practice against.

— Steve Sloan, on preparing for Clemson's 320-pound nose guard

Charles joined my family for a day at the beach and my children asked if they could go into the ocean. I had to tell them, "Not right now, kids. Charles is using it."

— Pat Williams, on 260-pound power forward Charles Barkley

Birds

Birds of a feather flock together . . . and then crap on your car.

— *Anonymous*

A bird in the hand . . . is going to poop on you.

— *Anonymous, first-grader finishing a popular saying*

Birthdays

When a man has a birthday he takes a day off, but when a woman has a birthday she takes a year off.

— *Anonymous*

The woman who puts the right number of candles on her birthday cake is playing with fire.

— *Anonymous*

An experienced husband is one who remembers his wife's birthday, but forgets which one it is.

— *Anonymous*

The best way to remember your wife's birthday is to forget it once.

— *E. Joseph Cossman*

Memory is what tells a man that his wife's birthday was yesterday.

— *Mario Rocco*

Blame

The man who smiles when things go wrong has thought of someone to blame.

— *Anonymous*

To err is human; to blame it on somebody else is even more human.

— *John Nadeau*

Blessings

What I'm looking for is a blessing that's not in disguise.

— *Kitty Collins*

Boats

The two happiest days in a man's life are the day he buys his boat and the day he sells it.

— *Luanne Rice*

Books

Literary critic: A person who can find a meaning in literature that the author didn't know was there.

— *Anonymous*

An encyclopedia is a system for collecting dust in alphabetical order.

— *Mike Barfield*

Book: Handy package containing varying amounts of low-grade toilet paper for emergency use on long hikes through the deep woods, at remote campsites or in poorly equipped lodges.

— *Henry Beard and Roy McKie*

One always tends to overpraise a long book, because one has got through it.

— *E.M. Foster*

Never lend books, for no one ever returns them; the only books I have in my library are books that other folks have lent me.

— *Anatole France*

Rare volume: A returned book.

— *Harry Herschelovitzer*

G.K. Chesterton was once asked what single book he would most like to have if he were stranded on a desert island. With typical wit, he replied, *Thomas' Guide to Practical Shipbuilding.*

— *Bruce Larson*

There are seventy million books in American libraries, but the one you want to read is always out.

— *Tom Masson*

Why pay a dollar for a bookmark? Use the dollar as a bookmark.

— *Fred Stoller*

Great Funny Quotes

Classic: A book which people praise and don't read.

— *Mark Twain*

I have hundreds of books, but no bookcase. Nobody would lend me a bookcase.

— *Henny Youngman*

Boots
Boot: A shallow puddle worn on the foot.

— *Henry Beard and Roy McKie*

Boredom
10 March . . . 0 hours climbing. Write five pages to my mother-in-law. Getting desperate.

— *Dave Johnson, journal entry, on sixth day stormbound on Mount Foraker, Alaska*

Bores
A bore is someone who talks about himself when you want to talk about yourself.

— *Robert Benson*

Bores bore each other too; but it never seems to teach them anything.

— *Don Marquis*

A bore is a person who can change the subject to his topic faster than you can change it back to yours.

— *Laurence Peter*

Bosses
A boss is someone who is early when you're late and late when you're early.

— *Anonymous*

A handicapped golfer is anybody who plays with his boss.

— *Anonymous*

The best incentive in business is the sound of the boss's footsteps.

— *Anonymous*

Tell your boss what you think of him, and the truth shall set you free.

— Anonymous

Push here for a word from the boss.

— Note on air hand dryer in restroom at work

The only time you play great golf is when you are doing everything within your power to lose to your boss.

— Henry Beard

A superior is not late, but held up, not asleep but resting, not wrong, but incorrectly briefed.

— Lev Kopelev

Accomplishing the impossible means only that the boss will add it to your regular duties.

— Doug Larson

To make a long story short, there's nothing like having the boss walk in.

— Doris Lilly

When bosses say "I want to know what you really think" they probably mean it. It's the moment after you tell them what you really think that the statement becomes a lie.

— Mark McCormack

I hate office politics. I just happen to enjoy mowing my boss's lawn on weekends.

— Gene Perret

The supervisor is a man who can bring gaiety, laughter and joy into the workplace . . . just by being absent.

— Gene Perret

I knew one boss who had a permanent sign on the wall behind his desk. It read: "Of course I want it today. If I wanted it tomorrow, I would have given it to you tomorrow."

— Gene Perret

The supervisor is the leader of the herd. When he's happy, his employees are happy. When he's upset, his employees are upset. When he's on vacation . . .

— *Gene Perret*

They say that crime doesn't pay, but it will if it goes to lunch with my boss.
— *Gene Perret*

Boxing
It's just a job. Grass grows, birds fly, waves pound the sand. I beat people up.
— *Muhammad Ali*

Flight attendant: "Mr. Ali, please fasten your seat belt."
     Muhammad Ali: "Superman don't need no seat belt."
     Flight attendant: "Superman don't need no airplane, either."
— *Anonymous*

I went to a fight the other night, and a hockey game broke out.
— *Rodney Dangerfield*

To me, boxing is like a ballet, except there's no music, no choreography and the dancers hit each other.
— *Jack Handey*

Getting hit.
— *Sugar Ray Robinson, on what he liked least about boxing*

Take boxing, the simplest, stupidest sport of all. It's almost as if these two guys are just desperate to compete with each other, but they couldn't think of a sport. So they said, "Why don't we just pound each other for 45 minutes? Maybe someone will come watch that."
— *Jerry Seinfeld*

I was once offered $300 to throw a fight in the third round but I had to turn it down because I had never made it to the third.
— *Lon Simmons, reflecting on a short career as a pro boxer*

Boys

Boy to mother: "You never mention the dirt I track out."

— *Anonymous*

Social security: When a boy has the only football or baseball in the neighborhood.

— *Anonymous*

A boy is a noise with some dirt on it.

— *Anonymous*

Home to a small boy is merely a filling station.

— *Anonymous*

It is a mistake to believe that because a boy is quiet, he is up to mischief; he may be asleep.

— *Anonymous*

Do you know what happens to little boys who keep interrupting? They grow up and make a fortune doing commercials on television.

— *Anonymous*

Two of my grandsons were playing marbles when a pretty little girl walked by. "I'll tell you," said Jake to JD, "when I stop hating girls, that's the one I'm going to stop hating first."

— *Anonymous*

My son, who is eleven, has started going to dance parties. Only minutes ago he was this little boy whose idea of looking really sharp was to have all the Kool-Aid stains on his He-Man T-shirt be the same flavor; now, suddenly, he's spending more time per day on his hair than it took to paint the Sistine Chapel.

— *Dave Barry*

A boy is someone who wants to grow up fast and be a fireman and eat candy for a living.

— *E.E. Brussell*

A boy is a hurry on its way to doing nothing.

— *John Ciardi*

A boy becomes an adult three years before his parents think he does, and about two years after he thinks he does.

— *Lewis Hershey*

Give a small boy a hammer and he will find that everything he encounters needs pounding.

— *Abraham Kaplan*

The *model boy* in my hometown has the admiration of all the mothers and the detestation of all their sons.

— *Mark Twain*

One of the hard things for parents to understand is how – if it takes the whole family one hour to get junior up and dressed and off to school in time, with only a slim chance of his remembering everything he's supposed to take – he can get dressed for a ball game, with no prompting, in ten minutes and be off without forgetting the minutest detail of his equipment.

— *Gluyas Williams*

Broadcasters
When you have dinner with Howard Cosell, he broadcasts the meal.

— *Woody Allen*

Broccoli
You can't hide a piece of broccoli in a glass of milk.

— *Armir, age nine*

Brothers
Older brothers invented terrorism. "Louie, see that swamp? There's a monster in it." So for years I walked way around it. Until I got a little older, a little wiser – and a little brother.

— *Louie Anderson*

Brothers and Sisters

Matthew knows what he would like to do but he's not sure where he could find a rocket that would shoot his sister Vanessa to Mars.

— *Paula Danziger*

One sister for sale!
    One sister for sale!
    One crying and spying young sister for sale!
    I'm really not kidding,
    So who'll start the bidding.

— *Shel Silverstein*

Budgets

Budget: A family quarrel.

— *Anonymous*

We are living in the kind of country where we find the average citizen is one who as soon as he is able to afford a Chevrolet buys a Cadillac.

— *Anonymous*

There are several ways in which to budget the family income, all of them unsatisfactory.

— *Robert Benchley*

Expenditures rise to meet income.

— *Cyril Parkinson*

Just about the time you think you can make both ends meet, somebody moves the ends.

— *Pansy Penner*

I like the housewife who had a simple reply to budgeting. She told the bank official who called, "I can't be overdrawn. I still have blank checks left."

— *Gene Perret*

I gave him an unlimited budget and he exceeded it.

— *Edward Williams*

Buildings

No exit: A sign indicating the most convenient way out of a building.

— *Anonymous*

PULL. If that doesn't work, PUSH. If that doesn't work, we're closed. Come again.

— *Vera Kasson, sign on a post office door*

Bull Riding

All there is to bull riding is to put one leg on each side of the bull and make an ugly face for eight seconds.

— *Jim Shoulders*

Bunk Beds

Never let a child wearing Superman pajamas sleep on the top bunk.

— *Anonymous*

Bureaucracy

Guidelines for Bureaucrats: 1) When in charge, ponder. 2) When in trouble, delegate. 3) When in doubt, mumble.

— *James Boren*

Paperwork is the embalming fluid of bureaucracy, maintaining an appearance of life where none exists.

— *Robert Meltzer*

It's a poor bureaucrat who can't stall a good idea until even its sponsor is relieved to see it dead and officially buried.

— *Robert Townsend*

Businesses

Batten, Barton, Durstine & Osborne – sounds like a trunk falling down a flight of stairs.

— *Fred Allen*

Business opportunities are like buses, there's always one coming.

— *Richard Branson*

Sorry about the crowding, but welcome to coach class.

— Mike DeWine, Ohio senator, to seven airline CEOs forced to sit in close quarters while testifying about antitrust legislation

I remember when we opened, we didn't have enough money to finish the landscaping and I had Bill Evans go out and put Latin tags on all of the weeds.

— Walt Disney

I think Pringles' initial intention was to make tennis balls. But on the day the rubber was supposed to show up, a big truckload of potatoes arrived instead.

— Mitch Hedberg

I like to buy a company any fool can manage because eventually one will.

— Peter Lynch

There are certain things that tax your credibility – like the fourth anniversary of a going-out-of-business sale.

— Robert Orben

We shake papers at each other the way primitive tribes shake spears.

— John Osborn, Jr.

Behind every genius in business is an assistant telling him which buttons to push to get the telephone to work.

— Gene Perret

I had one typewriter for fifty years, but I have bought seven computers in six years. I suppose that's why Bill Gates is rich, and Underwood is out of business.

— Andy Rooney

I asked my publisher what would happen if he sold all the copies of my book he had printed. He said, "I'll just print another ten."

— Eric Sykes

My gum company made a $40-million profit last year, and I can't get the financial writers to say a word about it. But I fire a manager and everybody shows up.

— *Phillip Wrigley*

Busses
Look at all the buses that want exact change. I figure if I give them exact change, they should take me exactly where I want to go.

— *George Wallace*

Busyness
If you want to find out how busy a man is, ask him to do something for you.

— *Anonymous*

No matter how busy people are, they are never too busy to stop and talk about how busy they are.

— *Anonymous*

Cabs
I saw today a cab driver take an elderly woman across the street. No, wait a minute, the word I'm looking for is . . . knock, knock her across.

— *David Letterman*

Caddies
Caddies are a breed of their own. If you shoot a 66, they say, "Man, we shot 66!" But go out and shoot 77, and they say, "Poor guy, he shot 77!"

— *Lee Trevino*

Calm
If you can keep your head when all about you are losing theirs, it's just possible you haven't grasped the situation.

— *Jean Kerr*

Camping
When using a public campground, a tuba placed on your picnic table will keep the sites on either side of you vacant.

— *Anonymous*

Campers: Nature's way of feeding mosquitoes.

— Anonymous

It always rains on tents. Rainstorms will travel thousands of miles, against prevailing winds, for the opportunity to rain on a tent.

— Dave Barry

I am not the type who wants to go back to the land – I am the type who wants to go back to the hotel.

— Fran Lebowitz

Camps

Not me, but some of the kids who have dogs did.

— Anonymous, little boy, when his parents asked him if he got homesick at camp

A camp is a summer place in the country where a mother sends her children for her vacation.

— Anonymous

Summer camp is where the parents spend a thousand dollars so their daughter can learn to make a fifty-cent potholder.

— Anonymous

Whoever said, "Money can't buy happiness," never sent his children to summer camp.

— Anonymous

Summer camps make a determined effort to hire staff members who meet the highest possible standards of maturity and responsibility. But eventually they give up and hire college students.

— Dave Barry

Careers

If you were a member of Jesse James' band and people asked you what you were, you wouldn't say, "Well, I'm a desperado." You'd say something like, "I work in banks," or "I've done some railroad work." It took me a long time just to say "I'm a writer."

— Roy Blount, Jr.

Most people work just hard enough not to get fired and get paid just enough not to quit.

— *George Carlin*

Never drink black coffee at lunch; it will keep you awake in the afternoon.
— *Jilly Cooper*

I'm a vice president in charge of sports marketing. That means I play golf and go to cocktail parties. I'm pretty good at my job.

— *Mickey Mantle*

I'm a doctor and picking up my five-year-old daughter, Chloe, from nursery one day, I left my bag and stethoscope on the back seat of my car. She started playing with the stethoscope and I began wondering, could my daughter be destined to follow in my footsteps? Then she spoke into the instrument, "Welcome to McDonald's. May I take your order?"

— *Mark Miller*

It's a recession when your neighbor loses his job; it's a depression when you lose yours.

— *Harry S. Truman*

Carrots
Carrots? Ugh! I don't know what company makes this stuff, but I hate it.
— *Dewey,* Malcolm in the Middle

Cars
The louder the car alarm, the more likely everyone but the owner will hear it.

— *Anonymous*

About the time you are pretty well satisfied with your progress, the Joneses buy a new car.

— *Anonymous*

Misery is seeing your car keys through a locked car window.
— *Anonymous*

Only a man would buy a $500 car and put a $4,000 stereo in it.

— *Anonymous*

Free rose for mother with gas.

— *Mother's Day gas station ad*

Never lend your car to anyone to whom you have given birth.

— *Erma Bombeck*

Nothing ages your car as much as the sight of your neighbor's new one.

— *Evan Esar*

The difference between estimated miles per gallon and what you actually get is about like the difference between salary and take-home pay.

— *Doug Larson*

When buying a used car, punch the buttons on the radio. If all the stations are rock 'n' roll, there's a good chance the transmission is shot.

— *Larry Lujac*

An optimist is a father who lets his teenager borrow the car. A pessimist is one who won't. A pedestrian is one who did.

— *Bob Monkhouse*

There is no limit to the amount of items that can be strapped to the roof of your car, providing you use the correct slipknots.

— *Kevin Nealon, on what his father taught him*

My car has this feature that I guess is standard, because it was on my last car too. It has a rotating gas tank. Whatever side of the pump I pull up to, it's on the other side.

— *Rita Rudner*

A father and his car keys are soon parted.

— *Pip Smart*

Home, nowadays, is a place where part of the family waits till the rest of the family brings the car back.

— *Earl Wilson*

If you care at all what the inside of your car looks like, you might want to think again about becoming a father.

— *Jason Wilson*

My wife called me. She said, "There's water in the carburetor." I said, "Where's the car?" She said, "In the lake."

— *Henny Youngman*

Cats

I named my kitten Rose – fur soft as a petal, claws sharper than thorns.
— *Astrid Alauda*

When your cat has fallen asleep on your lap and looks utterly content and adorable you will suddenly have to go to the bathroom.

— *Anonymous*

The little boy insisted he wasn't pulling the cat's tail. He was just holding it and the cat was pulling.

— *Anonymous*

Never try to baptize a cat.

— *Eileen, age eight*

The cat is above all things, a dramatist.

— *Margaret Benson*

As every cat owner knows, nobody owns a cat.

— *Ellen Berkeley*

I don't know if you've ever watched a cat try to decide where to sit, but it involves a lot of circling around, sitting, getting up again, circling some more, thinking about it, lying down, standing up, bathing a paw or tail and . . . circling.

— *Deborah and James Howe*

If there is another way to skin a cat, I don't want to know about it.
— *Steve Kravitz*

I've never understood why women love cats. Cats are independent, they don't listen, they don't come in when you call, they like to stay out all night, and when they're home they like to be left alone and sleep. In other words, every quality that women hate in a man, they love in a cat.

— *Jay Leno*

No matter how much cats fight, there always seem to be plenty of kittens.

— *Abraham Lincoln*

The best things in life really are free. So, how many kittens do you want?

— *Nancy Perdue*

We've got a cat called Ben Hur. We called it Ben till it had kittens.

— *Sally Poplin*

In ancient times, cats were worshipped as gods. They have never forgotten this.

— *Terry Pratchett*

The main advantage of working at home is that you get to find out what cats really do all day.

— *Lynne Truss*

Cats and Dogs

Dogs have Masters. Cats have staff.

— *Anonymous*

A dog will sit beside you while you work. A cat will sit on the work.

— *Pam Brown*

Dogs come when they're called; cats take a message and get back to you.

— *Missy Dizick*

Cats are smarter than dogs. You can't get eight cats to pull a sled through snow.

— *Jeff Valdez*

Celery

There ought to be some way to eat celery so it wouldn't sound like you were stepping on a basket.

— *Kin Hubbard*

Cement

Cement: The stuff that won't set until a dog or small boy runs through it.

— *Anonymous*

Cemeteries

Cemetery: An isolated spot, usually in the suburb, where mourners swap lies.

— *Ambrose Bierce*

Change

Change is good; you go first.

— *Tom McGehee*

Character

I heard Tonya Harding is calling herself the Charles Barkley of figure skating. I was going to sue her for defamation of character, but then I realized I have no character.

— *Charles Barkley*

Charisma

Charisma is what makes one man a skinny grandfather with bad teeth repeating the same story over and over since 1964 and another man Mick Jagger singing "Satisfaction" to a stadium full of screaming fans at three hundred bucks a head.

— *Dennis Miller*

Charmers

A beauty is a woman you notice, a charmer is one who notices you.

— *Adlai Stevenson*

Checking Accounts

Joint account: An account where one person does the depositing and the other the withdrawing.

— *Anonymous*

A joint account is never overdrawn by the wife. It's just underdeposited by the husband.

— *Anonymous*

Cheerfulness
Early morning cheerfulness can be extremely obnoxious.

— *William Feather*

Cheese Shredders
I have a cheese shredder at home, which is its positive name. They don't call it by its negative name, which is sponge ruiner.

— *Mitch Hedberg*

Chess
I had lunch with a chess champion the other day. I knew he was a chess champion because it took him twenty minutes to pass the salt.

— *Eric Sykes*

Chewing Tobacco
Never slap a man who's chewing tobacco.

— *Will Rogers*

Childproof
If you cannot open a childproof bottle, use pliers or ask a child.

— *Bruce Lansky*

Children
Ow: The first word spoken by children with older siblings.

— *Anonymous*

One thing you can say for kids, at least they don't bore you with cute things their parents said.

— *Anonymous*

I learned a long time ago that there are basically three ways to get things done. You can do it yourself, get someone else to do it or ask your children not to do it.

— *Anonymous*

The peak years of mental activity are between four and eighteen. At four, we know all the questions and at eighteen, we know all the answers.

— Anonymous

A little girl ran into the classroom and told the teacher, "Two boys are fighting out on the playground, teacher, and I think the one on the bottom would like to see you."

— Anonymous

By the time we realize our parents may have been right, we usually have children who think we are wrong.

— Anonymous

A man with no children misses a lot. For instance, a man with no children will never know the thrill of officiating at the funeral of a dead goldfish.

— Anonymous

One of our neighbor's kids does bird impressions. He eats worms.

— Anonymous

One day at work, while I was waiting on a customer, my colleague asked the customer's little boy how old he was. "I can't tell you," the child replied. "I have my mittens on."

— Anonymous

A person with six children is better satisfied than a person with six million dollars. The reason for this is that the man with six million dollars wants more.

— Anonymous

Queen Victoria: Queen Victoria was the longest queen who ever sat on a throne.

— Anonymous, child

Children should be seen and not . . . spanked or grounded.

— Anonymous, first-grader finishing a popular saying

"Darling, when was the last time we received a letter from our son?"
  "Just a second, I'll look in my checkbook."

— *Anonymous*

If you don't want your children to hear what you're saying, pretend you're talking to them.

— *Anonymous*

Parents are embarrassed when their children tell lies, and even more embarrassed when they tell the truth.

— *Anonymous*

How come dumb stuff seems so smart while you're doing it.

— *Dennis the Menace*

Don't squat with your spurs on.

— *Noronha, age thirteen*

Kids will go upstairs to fetch something you're too lazy to fetch yourself – just for the fun of the trip. Of course they never come back with the thing you actually wanted.

— *Anonymous*

When Tracy was eight, she would beat the best ladies at the local tennis club and then go over to the baby-sitting area and play in the sandbox.

— *Jeanne Austin, Tracy's mother*

You see much more of your children once they leave home.

— *Lucille Ball*

Mother Nature, in her infinite wisdom, has instilled within each of us a powerful biological instinct to reproduce; this is her way of assuring that the human race, come what may, will never have any disposable income.

— *Dave Barry*

No matter what stage your child is in, the parents who have older children always tell you the next stage is worse.

— *Dave Barry*

You should never have more children than you have car windows.
— *Erma Bombeck*

An advantage of having only one child is that you always know who did it.
— *Erma Bombeck*

We share the same genes, chromosomes and last name. We have never eaten the same breakfast cereal, watched the same TV shows, liked the same people or spoken the same language.
— *Erma Bombeck*

Youngsters of the age of two and three are endowed with extraordinary strength. They can lift a dog twice their own weight and dump him into the bathtub.
— *Erma Bombeck*

Kids will eat mud (raw or baked), rocks, paste, crayons, ballpoint pens, moving goldfish, cigarette butts and cat food. But try to coax a little beef stew into their mouths and they look at you like a puppy when you stand over him with the Sunday paper rolled up.
— *Erma Bombeck*

Then Trey told the lie that all parents-to-be have to tell themselves in order to have children: "Our kids will be different from everybody else's."
— *Carrie Bradshaw*

When you're eight years old, nothing is your business.
— *Lenny Bruce*

Because you are feeding both the child and the floor, raising this child will be expensive.
— *Bill Cosby*

The young always have the same problem – how to rebel and conform at the same time. They have now solved this by defying their parents and copying one another.
— *Quentin Crisp*

Many children threaten at times to run away from home. This is the only thing that keeps many parents going.

— Phyllis Diller

We spend the first twelve months of our children's lives teaching them to walk and talk and the next twelve years telling them to sit down and shut up.

— Phyllis Diller

Always be nice to your children because they are the ones who will choose your rest home.

— Phyllis Diller

If you don't have children the longing for them will kill you, and if you do, the worrying over them will kill you.

— Buchi Emecheta

There was never a child so lovely but that his mother was glad to get him to sleep.

— Ralph Waldo Emerson

Having one child makes you a parent; having two makes you a referee.

— David Frost

Having children gives your life purpose. Right now my purpose is to get some sleep.

— Reno Goodale

The beauty of *spacing* children many years apart lies in the fact that parents have time to learn the mistakes that were made with the older ones – which permits them to make exactly the opposite mistakes with the younger ones.

— Sydney Harris

The moment you have children yourself, you forgive your parents of everything.

— Susan Hill

Great Funny Quotes

"What time will dinner be tonight?" said Frances.

"Half past six," said Mother.

"Then I will have plenty of time to run away after dinner," said Frances.

— *Russell Hoban*

Don't take up a man's time talking about the smartness of your children; he wants to talk to you about the smartness of his.

— *Edgar Howe*

Dad, Denise pushed us out of the bathroom and Rudy doesn't have all of the shampoo rinsed out of her hair so if she goes blind can we get a dog?

— *Vanessa Huxtable,* The Cosby Show

The real menace in dealing with a five-year-old is that in no time at all you begin to sound like a five-year-old.

— *Jean Kerr*

Notoriously insensitive to subtle shifts in mood, children will persist in discussing the color of a recently sighted cement-mixer long after one's own interest in the topic has waned.

— *Fran Lebowitz*

Childhood is a time of rapid changes. Between the ages of twelve and seventeen, a parent can age thirty years.

— *Sam Levenson*

My three-year-old son turned to his five-year-old sister, and said, "Just you wait till I'm older than you!"

— *Wayne Lowe*

Adorable children are considered to be the general property of the human race. Rude children belong to their mothers.

— *Judith Martin "Miss Manners"*

Having children is like having a bowling alley installed in your brain.

— *Martin Mull*

The first child is made of glass, the second porcelain, the rest of rubber, steel and granite.

— Richard Needham

You know your children are growing up when they stop asking where they came from and refuse to tell you where they're going.

— P. O'Brien

The quickest way for a parent to get a child's attention is to sit down and look comfortable.

— Lane Olinghouse

Everybody knows how to raise children except the people who have them.

— P.J. O'Rourke

The best way to keep children home is to make it pleasant – and let the air out of the tires.

— Dorothy Parker

Sing out loud in the car even, or especially, if it embarrasses your children.

— Marilyn Penland

The one thing children wear out faster than shoes is parents.

— John Plomp

A mother's children are like ideas; none are as wonderful as her own.

— Chinese proverb

People talk vaguely about the innocence of a little child, but they take mighty good care not to let it out of their sight for twenty minutes.

— Saki

A two-year-old is like having a blender, but you don't have a top for it.

— Jerry Seinfeld

Sign you live with a preschooler: You don't know where your curling iron is, but last time it was lost you found it in the dryer, dressed in Barbie's wedding dress.

— Sandi Shelton

Children don't ask for things they don't want. They just don't want them after they get them.

— *Howard Stevens*

I learned a long time ago to hire assistant coaches with three kids. He'll be in his office working at eight every morning so he doesn't have to deal with getting the kids off to school.

— *Dick Versace*

In America the young are always ready to give to those who are older than themselves the full benefits of their inexperience.

— *Oscar Wilde*

Nathan Haley said, "I only regret that I have but one life to give for my country." This has come to be known as Haley's comment.

— *Larry Wolters, nine-year-old's answer on test*

Choirs
How do you join the choir?

You go into the church looking for the AA meeting and you go into the wrong room by mistake and they're so happy to see you that you don't dare leave.

— *Anonymous*

Chores
The best way to keep your kids out of hot water is to put some dishes in it.

— *Anonymous*

It is amazing how quickly the kids can learn to drive a car, yet are unable to understand the lawnmower, snowblower or vacuum cleaner.

— *Ben Berger*

My kids always perceived the bathroom as a place where you wait it out until all the groceries are unloaded from the car.

— *Erma Bombeck*

I've seen kids ride bicycles, run, play ball, set up a camp, swing, fight a war, swim and race for eight hours – yet have to be driven to the garbage can.

— *Erma Bombeck*

There are three ways to get something done: do it yourself, employ someone or forbid your children to do it.

— *Monta Crane*

My mother had an automatic garbage disposal. She would detect unerringly when you plan to go out and put the garbage bag in your hand to take with you.

— *Sam Levenson*

Any kid will run an errand for you if you ask at bedtime.

— *Red Skelton*

Christians

Christian: One who believes that the New Testament is a divinely inspired book admirably suited to the spiritual needs of his neighbor.

— *Ambrose Bierce*

Christmas

It's a good idea to send the kids to bed early on Christmas Eve. It gives fathers a few more hours to play with their toys.

— *Anonymous*

The year you stop believing in Santa Claus is the year you start getting clothes for Christmas.

— *Anonymous*

Mommy, how soon to Christmas?
    Not long. Why do you ask?
    I was wondering if it was near enough for me to start being good.

— *Anonymous*

And on Christmas morning, after the gifts have been opened, what are the kids doing? Playing with boxes and snapping the air pockets of plastic packing material.

— *Erma Bombeck*

Our children await Christmas presents like politicians getting election returns . . . the Uncle Fred precinct and the Aunt Ruth district still to come in.

— *Marcelene Cox*

An informal survey shows that what most people want for Christmas is two more weeks to prepare for it.

— *Bob Stanley*

Christmas Cards

No matter how many Christmas cards you send out, the first one you get is from someone you missed.

— *Anonymous*

Each year as we stamp and address them,
    And into each envelope stuff,
    At Christmas the very best card trick –
    Is simply just having enough.

— *Robert Orben*

Churches

He was of the faith chiefly in the sense that the church he currently did not attend was Catholic.

— *Kingsley Amis*

Lutherans get rid of squirrels by baptizing them and making them members. That way, they only see them on Christmas and Easter.

— *Anonymous*

Crying babies and disruptive children, like good intentions, should be carried out immediately.

— *Anonymous, preacher to the congregation*

The outreach committee has enlisted 25 members to make calls on people who are not afflicted with any church.

— *Church bulletin*

There will not be any Women Worth Watching this week.

— *Church bulletin*

Clergy Parking Space
You Park - You Preach

— *Sign outside of church*

Cigarettes

Cigarette sales would drop to zero overnight if the warning said "CIGA-RETTES CONTAIN FAT."

— *Dave Barry*

Cleaning

Keeping house is like threading beads on a string with no knot at the end.

— *Anonymous*

Frust: The small line of debris that refuses to be swept onto the dustpan and keeps backing a person across the room until she finally gives up and sweeps it under the rug.

— *Anonymous*

The average time between throwing something away and needing it badly is about two weeks.

— *Norman Bell*

There's something wrong with a mother who washes out a measuring cup with soap and water after she's only measured water in it.

— *Erma Bombeck*

It is better to light just one candle than to clean the whole apartment.

— *Eileen Courtney*

Cleaning your home while your kids are still growing is like shoveling the walk before it stops snowing.

— *Phyllis Diller*

If your children write their names in the dust on the furniture, don't let them put the year.

— *Phyllis Diller*

It's a small world, but not if you have to clean it.

— *Barbara Kruger*

Before the cleaning lady arrives, it is necessary to vacuum the entire house and straighten up all the rooms, because she works for friends of yours the other six days of the week and you don't want her to tell them how you really live.

— *P.J. O'Rourke*

I never get tired of housework – I don't do any. When guests come to visit, I just put out drop cloths and say we're painting.

— *Joan Rivers*

Clichés
Avoid clichés like the plague.

— *Samuel Goldwyn*

Clothes
Famous last words: Believe me, nobody'll dress up.

— *Anonymous*

A mother in Montana simply could not get her ten-year-old to tuck in his shirttails – until, one night, as he was sleeping, she sewed a lace edge on the bottom of each of his shirts.

— *Anonymous*

My wife has just two complaints: first, she's got absolutely nothing to wear. And second, she's run out of closet space to keep it in.

— *Anonymous*

Accessorize! Accessorize! Accessorize!
— *Anonymous, I learned all about life from a snowman*

Women don't dress to please men; if they did, they would dress a lot faster.
— *Anonymous*

I feel like such a failure. I've been shopping for over twenty years, and I still have nothing to wear.

— *Anonymous*

Nothing lasts as long as a suit you don't like.

— *Anonymous*

Although golf was originally restricted to wealthy Protestants, today it's open to anybody who owns hideous clothing.

— *Dave Barry*

I have always dressed according to certain Basic Guy Fashion Rules, including: both of your socks should always be the same color, or they should at least both be fairly dark.

— *Dave Barry*

Play It as It Lies is one of the fundamental dictates of golf. The other one is *Wear It if It Clashes.*

— *Henry Beard*

You know it's going to be a bad day when your teenager knocks on your bedroom door first thing in the morning and says, "Today is Nerd Day at school, Pop. Can I borrow some of your clothes?"

— *Ron Chapman*

I've got a shirt for every day of the week. It's blue.

— *Ron Dentinger*

Judge not a man by his clothes, but by his wife's clothes.

— *Lord Thomas Dewar*

The reason women don't play football is because eleven of them would never wear the same outfit in public.

— *Phyllis Diller*

Good-clothes sports.
    — *Billie Jean King, on the only sports in which women could participate: tennis, skating and golf*

When you're a kid, your mother's job is to make you look like a dork. The mittens pinned to your jacket, the Elmer Fudd earflap hat, the rubber boots with the Wonder bread bags over your feet. And, of course, the pièce de résistance, the snow pants. There's an outfit that screams, "Beat me up and take my lunch money!"

— *Dennis Miller*

When it comes to clothes, I never argue when our kids come back from the store with something that's garish, outlandish, bizarre, in bad taste and an affront to all normal sensibilities. I just say I like it. They take it back the next morning.

— *Robert Orben*

Weird clothing is *de rigueur* for teenagers, but today's generation of teens is finding it difficult to be sufficiently weird because the previous generation, who went through adolescence in the sixties and seventies, used up practically all the available weirdness.

— *P.J. O'Rourke*

Irony is when you buy a suit with two pairs of pants, and then burn a hole in the coat.

— *Laurence Peter*

When a woman tries on clothing from her closet that feels tight, she will assume she has gained weight. When a man tries on clothing from his closet that feels tight, he will assume the clothing has shrunk.

— *Rita Rudner*

A nun alone was a sailboat; two, side by side, a regatta; three, a whole armada. These sisters did not walk; they skimmed, they hovered.

— *Richard Selzer, on Sisters of Mercy in full habit*

They should put expiration dates on clothing so we men will know when they go out of style.

— *Gary Shandling*

Buying clothes a size too big only ensures that your kids will grow twice as fast.

— *Dee Ann Stewart*

Behind every successful man you'll find a woman who has nothing to wear.

— *James Stewart*

My kids learned how to operate a computer but never learned how to use a clothes hanger.

— *Andy Tate*

Have you ever taken anything out of the clothes basket because it had become, relatively, the cleaner thing?

— *Katherine Whitehorn*

Clubs

Exclusive club: A place where you can meet the kind of people you would have black-balled, if you'd have gotten in first.

— *Anonymous*

Coaches

Aren't all coaches interim coaches?

— *Wren Blair*

There are three things the average man thinks he can do better than everybody else: build a fire, run a motel and manage a baseball team.

— *Rocky Bridges*

If you're a pro coach, NFL stands for *Not For Long.*

— *Jerry Glanville*

It worries me that there's supposed to be two coaches meaner than I am. I would hate to have them start referring to me as "Good Old Woody."

— *Woody Hayes*

On this team, we're all united in a common goal: to keep my job.

— *Lou Holtz*

Howard Cosell coaches 28 NFL teams every week, so I figure I can coach one college team.

— *Joe Kapp, after being named head football coach at California without any previous coaching experience*

Coaches who start listening to fans wind up sitting next to them.

— *Johnny Kerr*

If he wanted me to run 26 miles through hills, I would. If he wanted me to carry water bottles, I would. If he wanted me to get my hair cut like his . . . well, you have to draw the line somewhere.

— *Babe Laufenberg, on Jimmy Johnson*

Great Funny Quotes

Why didn't you hit a home run like I told you to? If you're not going to do what I tell you, what's the use of me being manager?

— Groucho Marx, managing a celebrity softball team, to one of his players

If I'm half the coach on the bench that I was in the stands, we'll have no problems.

— Bob Plager

I quit coaching because of illness and fatigue. The fans were sick and tired of me.

— John Ralston

Managing is getting paid for home runs that someone else hits.

— Casey Stengel

I'm not sure whether I'd rather be managing or testing bulletproof vests.

— Joe Torre

Colleges

If I'm studying when you come back, please wake me.

— Anonymous, college student

Graduate school: The place where a young scholar goes off their parent's payroll – and on to their spouse's.

— Anonymous

In college, yuppies major in business administration. If to meet certain requirements they have to take a liberal arts course, they take Business Poetry.

— Dave Barry

I've attended several college orientation sessions with my son. As part of these sessions, the kids have interviews with college officials. My theory is that the officials close the door and say: "Relax. You'll spend the majority of college attending parties, playing Hacky Sack and watching *Friends*. The tour is purely for the parents. The guides make up the building names as they go along."

— Dave Barry

As he waved me off to college, I'll never forget my dad's parting words. He said, "Son, if there's anything you want, call me and I'll show you how to live without it."

— *Will Collins*

My daughter, aged seven, asked me what I did at work. I told her I worked at a college and my job was to teach people how to draw. She stared at me, incredulous, and said, "You mean they forgot?"

— *Howard Ikemoto*

I majored in eligibility.

— *Tim Laudner*

Son, it looks to me like you are spending too much time on one subject.
— *Shelby Metcalf, to a student who made four Fs and a D*

When I got the call two months ago to be your speaker, I decided to prepare with the same intensity many of you have devoted to an important term paper. So late last night, I began. I drank two cans of Red Bull, snorted some Adderall, played a few hours of Call of Duty, and then opened my browser. I think Wikipedia put it best when they said, "Dartmouth College is a private Ivy League university in Hanover, New Hampshire, United States." Thank you and good luck . . .
— *Conan O'Brien, opening remarks of his commencement speech at Dartmouth College*

Graduation speeches were invented largely in the belief that college students should never be released into the world until they have been properly sedated.

— *Gary Trudeau*

Economists report that a college education adds many thousands of dollars to a man's lifetime income – which he then spends sending his son to college.

— *Bill Vaughan*

Colorado
You carry your $3,000 mountain bike atop your $500 car.
— *Anonymous, You're in Colorado when . . .*

Comedy

The first rule of comedy is to never perform in a town where they still point at airplanes.

— Bobby Mills

Committees

Committee work is like a soft chair – easy to get into, but hard to get out of.

— Anonymous

A steering committee is a group of four people trying to park a car.

— Anonymous

Most people who join committees probably do so on the theory that it's easier to endorse an idea than to understand it.

— Anonymous

A committee is a cul-de-sac down which ideas are lured and then quietly strangled.

— Hilaire Belloc

Thou shalt not committee.

— Tal Bonham, eleventh commandment

When serving on a committee, never arrive on time; this stamps you as a beginner. Don't say anything until the meeting is half over; this stamps you as wise. Be as vague as possible; this avoids irritating the others. When in doubt, suggest a subcommittee be appointed. Be the first to move for adjournment; this will make you popular; it's what everyone is waiting for.

— Harry Chapman

A decision is what a man makes when he can't get anyone to serve on a committee.

— Fletcher Knebel

It is characteristic of committee discussions and decisions that every member has a vivid recollection of them and that every member's recollection differs violently from every other member's recollection.

— Jonathan Lynn and Anthony Jay

A committee is usually a group of uninformed, appointed by the unwilling to accomplish the unnecessary.

— *Syd Thrift*

Communication

Half the world is composed of people who have something to say and can't, and the other half who have nothing to say and keep on saying it.

— *Robert Frost*

We never talked, my family. We communicated by putting Ann Landers articles on the refrigerator.

— *Judy Gold*

There are certain phrases that, when you hear them, strike dread in your heart. One of these is: "Do you mind if I say something?" And another is the patent lie: "I'm not going to make a speech."

— *Joyce Grenfell*

What have you got when an Italian has one arm shorter than the other? A speech impediment.

— *Jackie Martling*

I know you believe you understand what you think I said, but I'm not sure you realize that what you heard is not what I meant.

— *Robert McCloskey*

Science may never come up with a better office communications system than the coffee break.

— *Gene Perret*

Making something perfectly clear only confuses everybody.

— *George Rockwell*

I like the way you always manage to state the obvious with a sense of real discovery.

— *Gore Vidal*

Competition

When I stopped swimming I started competing in other areas. I'd look at my husband and say, "I can make a pancake bigger and faster than you."
— *Amy Van Dyken*

This year we've got Nebraska right where we want them – off the schedule.
— *Cal Stoll*

Compliments

Some people pay a compliment as if they expect a receipt.
— *Kin Hubbard*

I simply cannot find the words to tell you how superb you were.
Try.
— *Claire Trevor and Judith Anderson*

Compromise

The man who says he is willing to meet you halfway is usually a poor judge of distance.
— *Anonymous*

Compromise: An arrangement whereby people who can't get what they want make sure nobody else does either.
— *Dick Cavett*

Computers

Thank you for calling the tech-support hotline. If your computer becomes obsolete while you're holding, press one to reach our sales department.
— *Anonymous*

To start press any key.
Where's the ANY key?
— *Anonymous, common query to computer helplines*

My software never has bugs – it just develops random features.
— *Anonymous*

Looking over the log book kept by the computer support staff at my office, I noticed several entries stating the problem was "PICNIC." I asked one of the technicians what PICNIC meant, and he laughed and reluctantly told me it meant "Problem In Chair, Not In Computer!"

— Anonymous

It's supposed to do that.

— Anonymous, computer help-line response

Hardware: Where the people in your company's software section will tell you the problem is.

— Dave Barry

Software: Where the people in your company's hardware section will tell you the problem is.

— Dave Barry

User: The word that computer professionals use when they mean *idiot.*

— Dave Barry

Experts agree that the best type of computer for your individual needs is the one that comes on the market about two days after you actually purchase some other computer.

— Dave Barry

Our newer, high-speed computer was in the shop for repair, and my son was forced to work on our old model with the black-and-white printer. "Mom," he complained to me one day, "this is like we're living back in the twentieth century."

— Denise Donavin

As anyone who has ever tried to purchase a PC knows, computer technology moves fast. No matter which computer you buy, no matter how much you spend, by the time you get it to your car – it's an eight-track tape player.

— Dennis Miler

A computer expert is someone who knows a lot of ways to say, "Well, then, let's try this."

— Gene Perret

Hardware is the part of the computer that can be kicked.

— *Jeff Pesis*

A computer once beat me at chess, but it was no match for me at kick boxing.

— *Emo Philips*

A modern computer is an electronic wonder that performs complex mathematical calculations and intricate accounting tabulations in one ten-thousandth of a second – and then mails out statements ten days later.

— *Paul Sweeney*

Concentration

I just try to concentrate on concentrating.

— *Martina Navratilova*

The least thing upset him on the links. He missed short putts because of the uproar of the butterflies in the adjoining meadows.

— *P.G. Wodehouse*

Concerts

The Quartet played Brahms last night at Carnegie Hall. Brahms lost.

— *Percy Hammond*

After conducting a concert in a small town, I once received the following note from a farmer who had attended the performance: "Dear Sir, I wish to inform you that the man who played the long thing you pull in and out only did so during the brief periods you were looking at him."

— *Arturo Toscanini*

Conclusions

A conclusion is the place where you get tired of thinking.

— *Martin Fischer*

Conferences

A conference is a gathering of important people who singly can do nothing, but together can decide that nothing can be done.

— *Fred Allen*

However momentous the conference, if it lasts long enough, the thought uppermost in the minds of the conferees is, "When do we eat?"

— *Anonymous*

A conference is a meeting held to decide when the next meeting will take place.

— *Anonymous*

Conference: The confusion of one man multiplied by the number present.

— *Anonymous*

Business conventions are important because they demonstrate how many people a company can operate without.

— *John Kenneth Galbraith*

I spoke to an attendee after one seminar. He said, "I still don't know anything, but I have a notebook to keep it in."

— *Gene Perret*

Confidence

Confidence is what you have when you don't really understand the situation.

— *Anonymous*

Confidence: That quiet assured feeling you have before you fall flat on your face.

— *L. Binder*

Conflict

Lady Astor and Churchill didn't get along. Lady Astor said to Churchill, "If you were my husband, I'd put arsenic in your tea."

He replied, "If you were my wife, I'd drink it."

— *Anonymous*

Cow dung at five feet.

— *Abraham Lincoln, on his choice of weapon when he was challenged to a duel*

When you see a married couple coming down the street, the one who is two or three steps ahead is the one that's mad.

— *Helen Rowland*

Congestion

The thing which in the subway is called congestion is highly esteemed in night spots.

— *Simeon Stunsky*

Conscience

Conscience is what makes a boy tell his mother before his sister does.

— *Anonymous*

A clear conscience is the sign of a bad memory.

— *Anonymous*

Consistency

Children are unpredictable. You never know what inconsistency they're going to catch you in next.

— *Franklin Jones*

Consultants

A consultant is a person who takes your money and annoys your employees while tirelessly searching for the best way to extend the consulting contract.

— *Scott Adams*

Consultation: To seek another's approval of a course already decided on.

— *Ambrose Bierce*

A consultant is someone who saves his client almost enough to pay his fee.

— *Arnold Glasgow*

A consultant is someone you pay a hundred dollars an hour to give you the same advice you ignore from your assistant.

— *Robert Orben*

Contracts

Knowledge is what you get from reading the small print in a contract; experience is what you get from not reading it.

— Anonymous

An oral contract isn't worth the paper it's written on.

— Samuel Goldwyn

Conversations

Intelligent conversationalist: One who nods his head in agreement while you're talking.

— Anonymous

It's good to hold a conversation. Just let go of it once in a while.

— Anonymous

Anyone who thinks the art of conversation is dead ought to tell a child to go to bed.

— Robert Gallagher

No man would listen to you talk if he didn't know it was his turn next.

— Edgar Howe

She plunged into a sea of platitudes, and with the powerful breast stroke of a channel swimmer made her confident way towards the white cliffs of the obvious.

— W. Somerset Maugham

Beware of the conversationalist who adds "in other words." He is merely starting afresh.

— Christopher Morley

The thoughtless are rarely wordless.

— Howard Newton

Trying to get a word in edgewise with some people is like trying to thread a sewing machine with the motor running.

— Bob Phillips

Conversation: Small talk between shots. If your partner's talking about someone who isn't around, it's gossip. If he's talking about himself, it's dull. If he's discussing your 250-foot drive, it's of paramount importance.

— *Martin Ragaway*

Please don't talk while I am interrupting.

— *Todd Rockefeller*

The trouble with her is that she lacks the power of conversation but not the power of speech.

— *George Bernard Shaw*

Cooking

Don't you think the Road Commissioner would be willing to pay my wife something for her recipe for pie crust?

— *Calvin Coolidge*

There is one thing more exasperating than a wife who can cook and won't, and that is the wife who can't cook and will.

— *Robert Frost*

I've been so busy, I don't even have time to cook for my kids. I don't wanna say we eat out a lot, but I've noticed that lately when I call my kids for dinner they run to the car.

— *Julie Kidd*

Courage

All of us have moments in our lives that test our courage. Taking children into a house with white carpet is one of them.

— *Erma Bombeck*

Cowards

Coward: One who in a perilous emergency thinks with his legs.

— *Ambrose Bierce*

Many would be cowards if they had courage enough.

— *Thomas Fuller*

Cows

Nature is amazing; who would have thought of growing a fly swatter on the rear end of a cow.

— Anonymous

When cows laugh, does milk come out of their noses?

— Jeff Marder

Credit Cards

My wife just underwent plastic surgery. I cut up her credit cards.

— Anonymous

I was feeling irritable and moody. It was that difficult time of the month when the credit card statement arrives.

— Julie Walters

Cricket

Cricket: A game which the English, not being a spiritual people, have invented in order to give themselves some conception of eternity.

— Stormont Mancroft

Crisis

There cannot be a crisis next week. My schedule is already full.

— Henry Kissinger

Criticism

I stopped criticizing my wife's cooking after her very first meal. I said, "How come you don't make the kind of pie filling my mother used to make?" And she said, "How come you don't make the kind of dough my father used to make?"

— Robert Orben

Dear Mrs. Jones:
    Thank you for your letter. I shall try to do better.
        — Carl Sandburg, form letter used for replying to critical letters

Crusaders

Crusaders: Fighting pilgrims to the Holy Land who wanted to find the Holy Grill. Many of them died of salvation.

— Anonymous, child

Dance

The hula dance is simple: you put some grass on one hip, some more grass on the other hip, and then you rotate the crops.

— Anonymous

When I dance, people think I'm looking for my keys.

— Ray Barone, Everybody Loves Raymond

In the Civil War Twist . . . the Northern part of you stands still while the Southern part tries to secede.

— Dick Gregory

Let's be honest: Isn't a lot of what we call tap dancing really just nerves?

— Jack Handy

I could dance with you until the cows come home. On second thought I'd rather dance with the cows until you come home.

— Groucho Marx

You go to the ballet and you see girls dancing on their tiptoes. Why don't they just get taller girls?

— Greg Ray

My father originated the limbo dance – trying to get into a pay toilet.

— Slappy White

Dating

Odds of meeting a single man: 1 in 23; a cute, single man: 1 in 529; a cute, single, smart man, 1 in 3,245,873; when you look your best, 1 in a billion.

— Lorna Adler

Dad to daughter's date: "She says she'll be right down. Care for a game of chess?"

— Anonymous

On the first date, they just tell each other lies, and that usually gets them interested enough to go for the second date.

— Mike, age ten, when asked what most people do on a date

It is the responsibility of the man to ask for the date, and the responsibility of the woman to think up excuses that get progressively more obvious until the man figures out that the woman would rather chew on a rat pancreas.

— Dave Barry

Dating simply means "going out with a potential mate and doing a lot of fun things that the two of you will never do again if you actually get married."

— Dave Barry

One way to find out if another person is *right* for you is to spend a lot of time with this person, talking and sharing experiences, so that you really get to know him or her as a human being. This is what we call the old-fashioned, or *stupid* way. The modern way is to take a Compatibility Quiz.

— Dave Barry

I don't have a girlfriend. But I do know a woman who'd be mad at me for saying that.

— Mitch Hedberg

A study shows men are hit by lightning four times as often as women. Usually after saying, "I'll call you."

— Jay Leno

The time had come to get rid of Henry at any cost. So I decided that the thing that discourages gentlemen more than anything else is shopping.

— Anita Loos

I spotted my ex-boyfriend at the mall. We had a really bad breakup, and I didn't want to make eye contact with him. Thank God I've had years of waitress training.

— Kate Mason

If you call a girl once and she doesn't return your call, it's possible that she never got the message. However, if you call a girl 51 times and she still hasn't called you back, it's you who hasn't gotten the message.

— *J. Chris Newberg*

Prom night was one of the worst nights of my life. My girlfriend looked fantastic . . . The problem was, so did her date.

— *Deion Sanders*

Going out with a jerky guy is kind of like having a piece of food caught in your teeth. All your friends notice it before you do.

— *Livia Squires*

I think my neighbor broke up with his girlfriend last night, because he played "Ain't No Sunshine When She's Gone," thirteen times in a row.

— *Wendy Wilkins*

My dental hygienist is cute. Every time I visit, I eat a whole package of Oreo cookies while waiting in the lobby. Sometimes she has to cancel the rest of her afternoon appointments.

— *Steven Wright*

Daughters

Don't think of it as losing a daughter. Think of it as gaining a bathroom.

— *Anonymous, overheard at a wedding*

The rich man and his daughter are soon parted.

— *Kin Hubbard*

Her mama said, "Don't eat with your fingers."
  "Okay," said Ridiculous Rose,
    So she ate with her toes!

— *Shel Silverstein*

One word of command from me is obeyed by millions, but I cannot get my three daughters to come down to breakfast on time.

— *Viscount Archibald Wavell*

Debt

Creditor: A man who has a better memory than a debtor.

— Anonymous

An acquaintance is a person whom we know well enough to borrow from, but not well enough to lend to.

— Ambrose Bierce

If you want the time to pass quickly, just borrow money for ninety days.

— R.B. Thomas

Things could be much worse. I could be one of my creditors.

— Henny Youngman

Decisions

My decision is maybe . . . and that's final!

— Sign on a businessman's desk

Defeat

If this is a blessing, it is certainly well disguised.

— Sir Winston Churchill, to his wife following defeat in 1945 election

Definitions

Indispensable man: The motorist who whizzes past you just as you spot a motorcycle cop in the rear view mirror.

— Anonymous

Once (adv.): Enough.

— Ambrose Bierce

Self-evident: Evident to one's self and to nobody else.

— Ambrose Bierce

Furbling: Having to wander through a maze of ropes at an airport or bank even when you are the only person in line.

— Rich Hall

Delegate

Good executives never put off until tomorrow what they can get someone else to do today.

— *Anonymous*

If you really want a job done, give it to a busy, important man. He'll have his secretary do it.

— *Calvin Coolidge*

Dentists

"How much will it cost to pull this tooth?"
   "Forty dollars."
   "What, for five minutes work?"
   "I'll work slower if you want."

— *Anonymous*

Desks

A desk is a wastebasket with drawers.

— *Anonymous*

A clean desk is a sign of a cluttered desk drawer.

— *Anonymous*

Diapers

A young couple bring their new baby home and the wife suggests that her husband try his hand at changing a diaper. "I'm busy," he says. "I'll do the next one." Next time the baby's diaper needs changing she asks him again. The husband says, "I didn't mean the next diaper. I meant the next baby."

— *Anonymous*

Any mother with half a skull knows that when Daddy's little boy becomes Mommy's little boy, the kid is so wet he's treading water.

— *Erma Bombeck*

Men who have fought in the world's bloodiest of wars are apt to faint at the sight of a truly foul diaper.

— *Gary Christenson*

Changing a diaper is a lot like getting a present from your grandmother – you're not sure what you've got but you're pretty sure you're not going to like it.

— *Jeff Foxworthy*

Eternal triangle: Diapers.

— *Leonard Levinson*

One of the most important things to remember about infant care is: never change diapers in midstream.

— *Don Marquis*

Dictionaries

The trouble with the dictionary is that you have to know how a word is spelled before you can look it up to see how it is spelled.

— *Will Cuppy*

Diets

Nothing tastes better than the stuff you're eating when you're cheating on your diet.

— *Anonymous*

Diet: A plan for putting off tomorrow what you put on today.

— *Ivern Ball*

The toughest part of dieting is not watching what you eat – it's watching what your friends eat.

— *Wilfred Beaver*

You know you're on a diet when cat food commercials make you hungry.

— *Andy Bumatai*

I've lost 2,000 pounds, but I've gained 2,200.

— *Billy Casper*

The toughest part of being on a diet is shutting up about it.

— *Gerald Nachman*

No matter what diet you are on, you can usually eat as much as you want of anything you don't like.

— *Walter Slezak*

Diplomacy

When a diplomat says "yes" he means "perhaps"; when he says "perhaps" he means "no"; when he says "no" he is no diplomat.

— *Anonymous*

Diplomat: A man who can convince his wife that a fur coat will make her look fat.

— *Anonymous*

Diplomacy: Telling your boss he has an open mind instead of telling him he has holes in his head.

— *Anonymous*

A diplomat is a man who always remembers a woman's birthday but never remembers her age.

— *Robert Frost*

There are two ironclad rules of diplomacy, but to one there is no exception. When an official reports that talks were useful, it can safely be concluded that nothing was accomplished.

— *John Kenneth Galbraith*

The chief distinction of a diplomat is that he can say no in such a way that it sounds like yes.

— *Lester Pearson*

Disability

I've decided to never sky dive. It would scare the heck out of my dog.
— *Gretchen Alexander, when asked if there is anything she wouldn't try as a blind woman*

Why do they put Braille dots on the keypad of the drive-up ATM?
— *Anonymous*

Met a guy this morning with a glass eye. He didn't tell me – it just came out in the conversation.

— *Jerry Dennis*

Discipline
My wife comes downstairs with a broken stick after spanking the kids. She throws it on the table and begins to talk out loud to . . . NOBODY!

— *Bill Cosby*

No matter how bad things get, a dad can always be counted on to say those words that immediately make it all better again – "Don't make me pull over!"

— *Suzanne Heins*

The child who is being raised strictly by the book is probably a first edition.

— *Aldous Huxley*

Divorce
Three of my wives were very good housekeepers. After we got divorced, they kept the houses.

— *Willie Pep*

Doctors
Eyedropper: A clumsy ophthalmologist.

— *Anonymous*

Doctors don't really prolong your life. But when you're stuck in the waiting room, it seems that way.

— *Gene Perret*

Dogs
Dachshund: An animal which is half a dog high by a dog and a half long.

— *Anonymous*

My dog, she looks at me sometimes with that look, and I think maybe deep down inside she must know exactly how I feel. But then maybe she just wants the food off my plate.

— *Anonymous*

Never buy a pit bull from a one-armed man.

> — *Anonymous*

Dachshund: A dog who wags his tail by remote control.

> — *Anonymous*

A dog's parents never visit.

> — *Anonymous, why some men have dogs and not wives*

Dogs don't notice if you call them by another dog's name.

> — *Anonymous, why some men have dogs and not wives*

Dogs like it if you leave a lot of things on the floor.

> — *Anonymous, why some men have dogs and not wives*

The later you are, the more excited your dogs are to see you.

> — *Anonymous, why some men have dogs and not wives*

You never have to wait for a dog; they're ready to go 24 hours a day.

> — *Anonymous, why some men have dogs and not wives*

Dogs agree that you have to raise your voice to get your point across.

> — *Anonymous, why some men have dogs and not wives*

A dog will not wake you up at night to ask, "If I died, would you get another dog?"

> — *Anonymous, why some men have dogs and not wives*

Never trust a dog to watch your food.

> — *Patrick, age ten*

GET A LONG LITTLE DOGGIE.

> — *Sign in a pet shop over the cage of dachshund puppies*

We will be back in five minutes. Sit! Stay!

> — *Sign at a veterinarian's office*

Dogs need to sniff the ground; it's how they keep abreast of current events. The ground is a giant dog newspaper, containing all kinds of late-breaking dog news items, which, if they are especially urgent, are often continued in the next yard.

— *Dave Barry*

Dogs feel very strongly that they should always go with you in the car, in case the need should arise for them to bark violently at nothing right in your ear.

— *Dave Barry*

You can say any foolish thing to a dog, and the dog will give you a look that says, "Wow, you're right! I never would've thought of that!"

— *Dave Barry*

A boy can learn a lot from a dog: obedience, loyalty and the importance of turning around three times before lying down.

— *Robert Benchley*

I have never stretched myself on a beach for an afternoon's nap that a dog, fresh from a swim, did not take up a position just to the left of my tightly closed eyes, and shake himself.

— *Robert Benchley*

Dachshunds are ideal dogs for small children, as they are already stretched and pulled to such a length that the child cannot do much harm one way or the other.

— *Robert Benchley*

The most affectionate creature in the world is a wet dog.

— *Ambrose Bierce*

Newfoundland dogs are good to save children from drowning, but you must have a pond of water handy and a child, or else there will be no profit in boarding a Newfoundland.

— *Josh Billings*

Did you ever notice when you blow in a dog's face, he gets mad at you, but when you take him in a car, he sticks his head out the window.

— *Steve Bluestein*

I know that dogs are pack animals, but it is difficult to imagine a pack of standard poodles . . . and if there were such a thing as a pack of standard poodles, where would they rove to? Bloomingdale's?

— *Yvonne Clifford*

Dogs show us their tongues as if they thought we were doctors.

— *Ramón Gómez de la Serna*

One good thing about a dark skirt is that it's the best thing for removing dog hair from the sofa.

— *Jane Goodsell*

He is so shaggy. People are amazed when he gets up and they suddenly realize they have been talking to the wrong end.

— *Elizabeth Jones*

Anybody who doesn't know what soap tastes like never washed a dog.

— *Franklin Jones*

A Canadian psychologist is selling a video that teaches you how to test your dog's IQ. Here's how it works: If you spend $12.99 for the video, your dog is smarter than you.

— *Jay Leno*

If you want to cure your dog's bad breath, just pour a little Lavoris in the toilet.

— *Jay Leno*

No one appreciates the very special genius of your conversation as a dog does. If you chat with him a while, gradually building up the argument and the intonation, he relishes it so that he will roll all around the floor, lie on his back kicking and groaning with joyous worship. Very few wives are so affected.

— *Christopher Morley*

A door is what a dog is perpetually on the wrong side of.

— *Ogden Nash*

Happiness to a dog is what lies on the other side of the door.

— Charlton Ogburn, Jr.

If you think dogs can't count, try putting three dog biscuits in your pocket and then giving Fido only two of them.

— Phil Pastoret

The best way to get a puppy is to beg for a baby brother – and they'll settle for a puppy every time.

— Winston Pendelton

All dogs know all about the Twilight Barking. It is their way of keeping in touch with distant friends, passing on important news, enjoying good gossip.

— Dodi Smith

My dog can bark like a congressman, fetch like an aide, beg like a press secretary, and play dead like a receptionist when the phone rings.

— Gerald Solomon

A well-trained dog will make no attempt to share your lunch. He will just make you feel so guilty that you will not enjoy it.

— Helen Thomson

Ever consider what our dogs must think of us? I mean, here we come back from a grocery store with the most amazing haul – chicken, pork, half a cow. They must think we're the greatest hunters on earth.

— Anne Tyler

Prince loved everything about my mother except her high-heeled shoes. When she dressed up, he would bark at her feet, and occasionally one of her shoes would turn up in a neighbor's flower bed.

— Thomas Wharton

Dreams

Now and then we had a hope that if we lived and were good, God would permit us to be pirates.

— Mark Twain, on his boyhood dreams

Drinks

A spilled drink flows in the direction of the most expensive object.

— *Jodi Briggs*

Driving

The shortest distance between two points is always under construction.

— *Noelie Alito*

Wife to husband: "I put a little scratch on the bumper, dear. If you want to look at it, it's in the backseat."

— *Anonymous*

A little girl asked her father, "Daddy, before you married Mommy, who told you how to drive?"

— *Anonymous*

Horn of plenty: Located in the car behind you.

— *Anonymous*

A shortcut is the longest distance between two points.

— *Anonymous*

Nothing improves a person's driving skills like the sudden discovery that his license has expired.

— *Anonymous*

Mommy, why do the idiots only come out when Daddy drives?

— *Anonymous*

Why is it that when you're driving and looking for an address, you turn down the volume on the radio?

— *Anonymous*

Many an accident occurs when a man is driving under the influence of his wife.

— *Anonymous*

A journey of a thousand miles begins with Dad saying, "I know a shortcut."

— *Anonymous*

If you want to be a leader with a large following, just obey the speed limit on a winding, two-lane road.

— *Charles Barr*

In most states you can get a driver's license when you're sixteen years old, which made a lot of sense to me when I was sixteen years old but now seems insane.

— *Dave Barry*

The best way to stop the noise in the car is to let her drive.

— *Milton Berle*

Can you abandon a child along a public highway for kicking Daddy's seat for 600 miles?

— *Erma Bombeck*

Have you noticed? Anyone driving faster than you is an idiot, and anyone driving slower than you is a moron.

— *George Carlin*

Never take a cross-country trip with a kid who has just learned to whistle.

— *Jean Deuell*

Despite what Ralph Nader says, the best safety device is a rearview mirror with a cop in it.

— *Bob Phillips*

In traffic there is only one rule that is constant: The lane of traffic that you are in is the lane of traffic that isn't moving.

— *Rita Rudner*

My parents had two constant arguments while they were driving: over how fast my father was going or how much gas was left in the tank. My father had a standard defense for either of these. It was always, "That's because you're looking at it from an angle. If you were over here, you'd see."

— *Jerry Seinfeld*

Couldn't I just leave $500 here on deposit?

> — *Clark Shaughnessy, after standing in a long line to pay one of many traffic tickets*

A lot of friction is caused by half the drivers trying to go fast enough to thrill their girlfriends and the other half trying to go slow enough to placate their wives.

> — *Bill Vaughan*

Drums

The first thing a child learns after he gets a drum is that he's never going to get another one.

> — *Anonymous*

Dust

Dust is a protective coating for the furniture.

> — *Mario Buatta*

Dyslexia

It's not easy having dyslexia. Last week I went to a toga party as a goat.

> — *Arthur Smith*

Eating

Meal time is the only time in the day when children resolutely refuse to eat.

> — *Fran Lebowitz*

Doctors will tell you that if you eat slowly you will eat less. Anyone raised in a large family will tell you the same thing.

> — *Sam Levenson*

A luncheon is a lunch that takes an eon.

> — *Judith Martin "Miss Manners"*

You do not sew with a fork, and I see no reason why you should eat with knitting needles.

> — *Miss Piggy, on chopsticks*

To try and get my kid to eat I'd sometimes say, "Just pretend it's sand."

> — *Michael Todd*

An Irish farmer, to cover the possibility of unexpected visitors, can often be found eating his dinner out of a drawer.

— *Niall Toibin*

Eating Out
It may be expensive to reach for the check, but it gets you home earlier.

— *Anonymous*

Economical
Spare no expense to make everything as economical as possible.

— *Samuel Goldwyn*

Economists
Economics: The science of telling you things you've known all your life, but in a language you can't understand.

— *Dick Armey*

You can generally tell whether a man is an economist by the number of times he uses the phrase: "All other things being equal."

— *William Davis*

There are three kinds of economist: those who can count and those who can't.

— *Eddie George*

If economists were any good at business, they would be rich men instead of advisers to rich men.

— *Kirk Kerkorian*

Two Americans have been awarded the Nobel Prize for Economics. They are the first to figure out all the charges on their phone bill.

— *Jay Leno*

Economists are people who see something work in practice and wonder if it would work in theory.

— *Ronald Reagan*

Wall Street indexes predicted nine out of the last five recessions.

— *Paul Samuelson*

If all economists were laid end to end, they would not reach a conclusion.

— *George Bernard Shaw*

Ecstasy

Ecstasy: Discovering a second layer of chocolates under the first.

— *Anonymous*

Editors

Editor: A person employed on a newspaper whose business is to separate the wheat from the chaff and see that the chaff is printed.

— *Elbert Hubbard*

Education

Education today is teaching a child how to talk and then teaching it how to keep quiet.

— *Anonymous*

Education is something you get when your folks send you to college. But it isn't complete until you've sent your own kids.

— *Anonymous*

Parents should conduct their arguments in quiet, respectful tones, and in a foreign language. You'd be surprised what an inducement that is to the education of children.

— *Judith Martin "Miss Manners"*

Efficiency

An efficiency expert is a man who believes in economy at any cost.

— *Anonymous*

Ego

An egotist is a person of low taste, more interested in himself than in me.

— *Ambrose Bierce*

The nice thing about egoists is that they don't talk about other people.

— *Lucille Harper*

But enough of me. Let's talk about you. What do you think of me?

— *Ed Koch*

Electricity

I had all my electric cords shortened to save on electricity.

— *Gracie Allen*

Eloquence

Eloquence: The ability to describe Pamela Anderson without using one's hands.

— *Michael Harkness*

Employees

Everything is relative: You're expendable when you ask for a raise but indispensable when you ask for a day off.

— *Anonymous*

"Yes," said the personnel manager to the job applicant, "what we're after is a man of vision; a man with drive, determination, fire; a man who can inspire others; a man who can pull our bowling team out of last place."

— *Anonymous*

In case of fire, flee the building with the same reckless abandon that occurs each day at quitting time.

— *Sign on employee bulletin board*

Statistics show that attendance at work is better among married men with children and spikes even higher among fathers of newborns.

— *Thomas Hill*

No man goes before his time. Unless, of course, the boss leaves early.

— *Frances Merron*

I had one worker who steadfastly refused to take a morning coffee break. He claimed it kept him awake all afternoon.

— *Gene Perret*

My boss used to tell the Personnel Manager to consider job applicants as carefully as if he were going to marry them. He used to tell him that until he met the Personnel Manager's wife.

— *Gene Perret*

Engineers

Normal people believe that if it ain't broke, don't fix it. Engineers believe that if it ain't broke, it doesn't have enough features yet.

— Scott Adams

Epitaphs

May my husband rest in peace till I get there.

— Dame Edna Everage

Equality

What makes equality such a difficult business is that we only want it with our superiors.

— Henry Becque

Eternity

Nothing lasts forever – with the exception of public broadcasting pledge week.

— Anonymous

Euphemisms

"We must do lunch sometime" is the polite euphemism for, "I don't care if I never see you again."

— Marcus Hunt

Evil

Good often comes from evil: the apple that Eve ate has given work to thousands of designers and dressmakers.

— Anonymous

Example

Few things are harder to put up with than the annoyance of a good example.

— Mark Twain

Executives

If things get worse, I will have to ask you to stop helping me.

— Sign on an executive's desk

A real executive goes around with a worried look on his assistants.

— Vince Lombardi

Executive: A guy who talks business on the golf course and golf at his business.

> — *Martin Ragaway*

Exercise
I swam ten laps
    I ran three miles
    I biked seven miles . . .
    It's been a good year!

> — *Anonymous*

She had joined a health club, once, but was so exhausted by the time she'd pulled herself into those awful leotards, she went home to bed.

> — *Fannie Flagg*

When purchasing exercise equipment, make sure it is of sturdy construction and that there is enough space to hang all your wet washing on it.

> — *Jeff Green*

My favorite machine at the gym is the vending machine.

> — *Caroline Rhea*

Experience
When a man with money meets a man with experience, the man with experience ends up with the money and the man with the money ends up with the experience.

> — *Anonymous*

Experience is what causes a person to make new mistakes instead of old ones.

> — *Anonymous*

Experience is often what you get when you are expecting something else.
> — *Anonymous*

Experience is a wonderful thing. It enables you to recognize a mistake when you make it again.

> — *Anonymous*

Experience is something I always think I have until I get more of it.

— *Burton Hillis*

Experience may be the best teacher but the one I had in grammar school was much prettier.

— *Don McNeill*

Experience is what you get when you don't get what you want.

— *Dan Stanford*

Good judgment is the result of experience, and experience is the result of bad judgment.

— *Walter Wriston*

Experts

Specialist: A generalist with a smaller practice and a larger home.

— *Anonymous*

Expert: One who knows all the answers, if you ask the right questions.

— *Anonymous*

An expert is a man who has made all the mistakes which can be made in a very narrow field.

— *Niels Bohrs*

An expert is somebody who is more than fifty miles from home, has no responsibility for implementing the advice he gives, and shows slides.

— *Ed Meese*

Extravagance

An extravagance is anything you buy that is of no earthly use to your wife.

— *Franklin Adams*

Face Lifts

A face lift will take twenty years off a person's age. But you can't fool a long flight of stairs.

— *Anonymous*

Faith

Tell a man that there are 500 billion stars in the universe and he will believe you. Tell him a fence has just been painted and he has to touch it to find out that it has been.

— *Herb Cohen*

Fame

Sometimes I'll get recognized out somewhere and then the next question they ask me is what I do.

— *Andre Agassi*

A celebrity is a person who works all his life to become known, then wears dark glasses to avoid being recognized.

— *Fred Allen*

Glory is fleeting, but obscurity is forever.

— *Napoléon Bonaparte*

After a fellow gets famous, it doesn't take long for someone to bob up that used to sit by him at school.

— *Kin Hubbard*

The main advantage of being famous is that when you bore people at dinner parties they think it is their fault.

— *Henry Kissinger*

Somebody asked if we were going to do something special. I said Joe already has a state named after him.
— *John Moreschi, Mayor of Joe Montana's hometown in Pennsylvania*

Once, I walked out of a bathroom stall at O'Hare Airport, and three women applauded. That's when I knew: I am famous.

— *Oprah Winfrey*

Family

When I was a boy, my family took great care with our snapshots. We posed in front of expensive cars and homes that weren't ours. We borrowed dogs.

Almost every family picture taken of us when I was young had a different borrowed dog in it.

— *Richard Avedon*

A family is a group of people who each like different breakfast cereal.

— *Milton Berle*

The other night I ate at a real nice family restaurant. Every table had an argument going.

— *George Carlin*

A family is a social unit where the father is concerned with parking space, the children with outer space and the mother with closet space.

— *Evan Esar*

You're probably a redneck if your family tree doesn't fork.

— *Jeff Foxworthy*

I didn't hire Scott because he's my son. I hired him because I'm married to his mother.

— *Frank Layden*

This book is dedicated to my mother, Mrs. Frieda Seidman; to my daughters, Laurie Jo and Mona Helene; and to my wife Sylvia. All equally dear to me, but for safety's sake listed here alphabetically according to first name.

— *Gerald Lieberman*

Nothing in life is *fun for the whole family.*

— *Jerry Seinfeld*

I'm Charley's aunt from Brazil – where the nuts come from.

— *Brandon Thomas*

Fans

Whenever I go to a ball game, I always end up in the same seat – between the hot dog vendor and his best customer.

— *Anonymous*

A baseball fan has the digestive apparatus of a billy goat. He can, and does, devour any set of diamond statistics with insatiable appetite and then nuzzles hungrily for more.

— *Arthur Daley*

I know why they threw it at me. What I can't figure out is why they brought it to the ball park in the first place.

— *Ducky Medwick, after a barrage of fruit, garbage and cardboard boxes from fans forced him to leave the seventh game of the 1934 World Series*

Why certainly I'd like to have that fellow who hits a home run every time, who strikes out every opposing batter and who throws strikes to any base or the plate when he's playing outfield. Any manager would want a guy like that playing for him. The only trouble is to get him to put down his cup of beer and come down out of the stands and do those things.

— *Danny Murtaugh*

My definition of a fan is the kind of guy who will scream at you from the sixtieth row of the bleachers because he thinks you missed a marginal holding call in the center of the interior line, and then after the game won't be able to find his car in the parking lot.

— *Jim Tunney, referee*

Farms
Farm: What a city man dreams of at 5:00 p.m., never at 5:00 a.m.

— *Anonymous*

Fashion
Heaven knows, I try to bend the dictates of fashion, but I'm a loser. When I grew my own bustle, they went out of style.

— *Erma Bombeck*

I base most of my fashion taste on what doesn't itch.

— *Gilda Radner*

Fashion is what one wears oneself. What is unfashionable is what other people wear.

— *Oscar Wilde*

Fathers

When your dad is mad and asks you, "Do I look stupid?" don't answer.

— *Hannah, age nine*

Can I go outside and help Daddy put snow chains on the car? I know all the words.

— *Anonymous, little boy to his mother*

A father is first a curiosity, then an amusement-park ride, then a referee and finally a bank.

— *Anonymous*

When you want to do something and you're not sure your dad will let you, ask him while he's asleep.

— *Anonymous, age eleven*

Pas de deux: father of twins.
    Coup de grace: lawnmower.

— *Anonymous*

A father is someone who carries pictures where his money used to be.

— *Anonymous*

Is there any sound more terrifying on a Sunday afternoon than a child asking, "Daddy, can we play Monopoly?"

— *Jeremy Clarkson*

Fatherhood is pretending the present you love most is soap-on-a-rope.

— *Bill Cosby*

A father can sound convincing when he says that he is delighted to have another bottle of Old Spice because he is down to his last six.

— *Bill Cosby*

This is the hardest truth for a father to learn: that his children are continuously growing up and moving away from him (until, of course, they move back in).

— *Bill Cosby*

It doesn't make any difference how much money a father earns, his name is always Dad-Can-I. Like all other children, my five have one great talent: they are gifted beggars. Not one of them ever ran into the room, looked up to me, and said, "I'm really happy that you're my father, and as a tangible token of my appreciation, here's a dollar."

— *Bill Cosby*

"What in the world are you doing down there?" Mom would shout down to the basement. "Just tinkering," would come Dad's response. He'd be happily rearranging empty paint cans, sorting rusty bent nails from not-so-rusty bent nails and contemplating exactly where to put up a set of shelves.

— *Allen Delaney*

At age eighteen, everybody thinks they know what's best. By the time you realize what your father was telling you was true, your own kids are telling you you're wrong.

— *Wayne Gretzky*

Fathers are what give daughters away to other men who aren't nearly good enough so they can have grandchildren that are smarter than anybody's.

— *Paul Harvey*

You know you've turned into your dad the day you put aside a thin piece of wood specifically to stir paint with.

— *Peter Kay*

Dad taught us what it takes to get things done – Mom's permission.

— *Kevin Kinzer*

Father's Day is like Mother's Day, except the gift is cheaper.

— *Gerald Lieberman*

I have two-year-old twins in my house. It's nuts. I make excuses to get out. "Honey, you need anything from anywhere? Anything from the Motor Vehicle Bureau? C'mon, let me register something. I was going out anyway, to apply for jury duty. Please!"

— *Ray Romano*

Not every dad can actually hear eyes rolling behind his back . . . but my dad could.

— *Dan Taylor*

When I was a boy of fourteen, my father was so ignorant I could hardly stand to have the old man around. But when I got to be 21, I was astonished at how much the old man had learned in seven years.

— *Mark Twain*

By the time a man realizes that maybe his father was right, he usually has a son who thinks he's wrong.

— *Charles Wadsworth*

There's nothing like being a dad. Though shoveling money down a bottomless hole comes close.

— *Myra Zirkle*

Faults
Never exaggerate your faults. Your friends will attend to that.

— *Robert Edwards*

The faults of others console us in our own.

— *Paul Eldridge*

To find out a girl's faults, praise her to her girlfriends.

— *Benjamin Franklin*

We only confess our little faults to persuade people that we have no big ones.

— *François de La Rochefoucauld*

Fear
I discovered I scream the same way whether I'm about to be devoured by a Great White or if a piece of seaweed touches my foot.

— *Kevin James*

Everyone has some fear. A man who has no fear belongs in a mental institution. Or on special teams.

— *Walt Michales*

Feedback

Feedback: The result when a baby doesn't appreciate the strained carrots.

— *Anonymous*

Files

We've got 25 years' worth of files out there, just sitting around. Now what I want you to do is go out there and throw everything out – but make a copy of everything first.

— *Samuel Goldwyn*

Everything can be filed under miscellaneous.

— *George Bernard Shaw*

A filing cabinet is a place where you can lose things systematically.

— *T.H. Thompson*

Fine Print

Education is when you read the fine print; experience is what you get when you don't.

— *Pete Seeger*

Firing

Fireproof: Being related to the boss.

— *Anonymous*

What am I going to do with all the orange clothes I bought?

— *Abe Lemons, on being fired as Texas coach*

They broke it to me gently. The manager came up to me before a game and told me they didn't allow visitors in the clubhouse.

— *Bob Uecker*

Fishing

The two best times to fish are *right before you get there; and right after you leave.*

— *Anonymous*

In telling fish tales, the first liar doesn't have a chance.

— *Anonymous*

My rod and my reel, they comfort me.

— *Anonymous*

Ferrule: Hardware fitting used to join together rod sections, consisting of a metal plug (male end) and a corresponding socket (female end) that are prone to a sudden, messy divorce during casts but invariably mate for life at the end of a long day of fishing.

— *Henry Beard and Roy McKie*

Fighting chair: Elaborate swivel-mounted seat in the stern of a deep-sea fishing boat in which a saltwater angler frantically pumping and reeling a hooked fish struggles with an overpowering urge to go to the bathroom.

— *Henry Beard and Roy McKie*

Knot: A tangle with a name.

— *Henry Beard and Roy McKie*

Hook: Irritating but highly reliable device used to quickly and precisely locate the position of one's thumb at the bottom of a tackle box.

— *Henry Beard and Roy McKie*

License: Permit issued upon payment of a modest fee that allows fishermen to lose lures in a specified area.

— *Henry Beard and Roy McKie*

Line: Length of long, thin, strong synthetic material stretched between two fishing rods and joined at its midpoint by a pair of linked hooks.

— *Henry Beard and Roy McKie*

Mummichog: 1) Popular baitfish also known as killifish. 2) Disappointing sound made by the outboard motor on the 31st through 500th attempt to start it.

— *Henry Beard and Roy McKie*

Wahoo: 1) Saltwater game fish similar to Spanish mackerel. 2) Remark made by angler who inadvertently sits on a treble-hooked saltwater fishing lure.

— *Henry Beard and Roy McKie*

Perch: 1) Popular panfish found in a number of habitats. 2) Standing place, such as a slippery bank, wet rock or rickety dock, from which an angler was fishing for perch shortly before he unexpectedly entered his prey's habitat.

— *Henry Beard and Roy McKie*

Rod: Flexible, tapered stick that is the basic tool of angling. A rod of even medium length is awkward to carry, but anglers have found through long experience that it can be easily shortened with an ordinary car door, station wagon tailgate or trunk lid.

— *Henry Beard and Roy McKie*

My biggest worry is that my wife [when I'm dead] will sell my fishing gear for what I said I paid for it.

— *Koos Brandy*

Even accountants are known, in their capacity as fishermen, blissfully to ignore differences between seven and ten inches, half a pound and two pounds, three fish and a dozen fish.

— *William Fox*

The Lord created the world two-thirds water and one-third land, with the obvious intention that man should spend two-thirds of his time fishing and one-third working.

— *Orville Freeman*

There is no greater fan of fly-fishing than the worm.

— *Patrick McManus*

The curious thing about fishing is you never want to go home. If you catch something, you can't stop. If you don't catch anything, you hate to leave in case something might bite.

— *Gladys Taber*

Flashlights

Flashlight: A mechanical device used by people to carry around dead batteries.

— *Anonymous*

Flattery

An amateur is a young man who, when flattering women, is afraid of overdoing it.

— *Anonymous*

Flatterer: One who convinces you that you are not alone in the way you feel about yourself.

— *Anonymous*

The aim of flattery is to soothe and encourage us by assuring us of the truth of an opinion we have already formed about ourselves.

— *Edith Sitwell*

Flying

I'm a nervous flyer, and it doesn't make it any easier when I get to the airport and see the sign TERMINAL.

— *Anonymous*

Airline pilots: Encourage your passengers to "get up and move about a bit" while doing 500 mph, 30,000 feet above an ocean, but indignantly insist they "remain seated with their seatbelts fastened" as you dawdle the three miles across the tarmac to the arrival gate at five mph.

— *Anonymous*

Try flying on any plane with a baby if you want a sense of what it must have been like to be a leper in the fourteenth century.

— *Nora Ephron*

Gunter's Second Law of Air Travel: The strength of the turbulence is directly proportional to the temperature of the coffee.

— *Nicholas Gunter*

My fear of flying starts as soon as I buckle myself in and the guy up front mumbles a few unintelligible words. Then before I know it, I'm thrust into the back of my seat by acceleration that seems way to fast, then we veer immediately into a turn that seems way too sharp, and the rest of the trip is an endless nightmare of turbulence and near-misses . . . then the cabbie drops me off at the airport.

— *Dennis Miller*

The best way to assure that your flight will leave on time is to arrive two minutes late.

— *Gene Perret*

When I left Pullman International Airport in Washington, I asked the baggage handler to send one bag to Seattle, one to Portland and the other to Billings, Montana. He said, "I can't do that." I said, "Why not? You did it two years ago."

— *George Raveling*

Focus Groups

Focus Groups are people who are selected on the basis of their inexplicable free time and their common love of free sandwiches.

— *Scott Adams*

Food

This stuff tastes awful. I could have made a fortune selling it in my health food store.

— *Woody Allen*

Inside me lives a skinny woman crying to get out. But I can usually shut her up with cookies.

— *Anonymous*

When somebody eats something that they think has gone bad, why do they always want you to taste it?

— *Anonymous*

My next house will have no kitchen – just vending machines.

— *Anonymous*

How'd they ever come up with that great plastic wrap that sticks to the food but not the bowl?

— *Anonymous*

Toddlers are more likely to eat healthy food if they find it on the floor.

— *Fran Blaustone*

My children refused to eat anything that hadn't danced on TV.

— *Erma Bombeck*

As a child my family's menu consisted of two choices: take it, or leave it.

— *Buddy Hackett*

I think they should put a warning label on strawberries: Caution – tastes nothing like a strawberry milkshake.

— *Ryan Kaplan*

It is no use trying to empty a sugar bag. You will always hear more sugar rattling around inside an empty sugar bag. Just throw it away.

— *Miles Kington*

Last night I had a typical cholesterol-free dinner: baked squash, skimmed milk and gelatin. I'm sure this will not make me live any longer, but I know it's going to seem longer.

— *Groucho Marx*

Animal crackers, and cocoa to drink,
    That is the finest of suppers, I think;
    When I'm grown up and can have what I please
    I think I shall always insist upon these.

— *Christopher Morley*

When it comes to foreign food, the less authentic the better.

— *Gerald Nachman*

If you believe no two women think alike, you've never been to a potluck dinner.

— *Bob Phillips*

Her favorite food is seconds.

— *Joan Rivers*

The biggest seller is cookbooks and the second is diet books – how not to eat what you've just learned how to cook.

— *Andy Rooney*

My doctor told me to stop having intimate dinners for four. Unless there are three other people.

— *Orson Welles*

Foolproof
It is impossible to make anything foolproof because fools are so ingenious.

— *Anonymous*

Football
When he says, "Sit down!" I don't even look for a chair.

— *Anonymous, on Vince Lombardi*

My wife calls me "much maligned." She thinks that's my first name. Every time she reads a story about me, that's always in front of my name.

— *Chris Bahr*

It's the one where the player pitches the ball back to the official after scoring a touchdown.

— *Bear Bryant, on his favorite move*

Football is not a contact sport. Football is a collision sport. Dancing is a contact sport.

— *Duffy Daugherty*

I've been asked to make a speech about my football team. My football team that just won nine games. My football team that just won the Rose Bowl. My football team that – I'm sorry, I forgot this wasn't my football team. It really belongs to you. Last year when we won only three and lost five, that was my football team.

— *Duffy Daugherty*

Our definition of quick hands was a guy who could steal hubcaps off a car that was moving.

— *Mike Ditka*

I'm probably about a 4.9 normally, but when a 280-pound guy is chasing me – I'm a 4.6.

— *John Elway, on the forty-yard dash*

I don't know – I only played there nine years.

— *Walt Garrison, when asked if Tom Landry ever smiled*

I recruited a Czech kicker, and during the eye examination the doctor asked if he could read the bottom line. The kicker said, "Read it? I know him."

— *Woody Hayes*

I don't mind starting a season with unknowns. I just don't like finishing a season with a bunch of them.

— *Lou Holtz*

We will get the heart and soul of our football team from the state of Minnesota. However, we'll have to go elsewhere for the arms and legs.

— *Lou Holtz*

I can't wait to get back to the restaurant and see the waiter who said, "Cheerios and Notre Dame are different: Cheerios belong in a bowl."

— *Lou Holtz, after Notre Dame upset Florida in the 1992 Sugar Bowl*

She was wrong. By the end of the season I'd sold our stereo, our car, the jewels and our television.

— *Lou Holtz, on his wife's prediction that he wouldn't sell anything if he took a part-time job selling cemetery plots*

My dad was in a circus act when I was a kid. He got shot out of a cannon. I'm an offensive lineman in the NFL. Sometimes I figure it would have been safer to have gone into the family business.

— *Bob Kuechenberg*

A runner must understand that there's one bad thing about carrying that football – it attracts a crowd.

— *John McKay*

It's like riding a bike on the freeway with cars coming at you.

— *Chris Miller, when asked if rejoining the NFL after a three-year layoff was like getting back on a bicycle*

Super Bowl Sunday is the one day of the year where everyone in the country, regardless of their religious beliefs, completely stops what they're normally doing. Especially the team I'm rooting for.

— Dennis Miller

Every time I went into the line on a fake I shouted, "I don't have it!"

— Bob Newhart, on being a high school running back

My wife has developed a very explicit way of indicating she's had enough of my watching football on TV. Last Saturday she went up to the set, pointed to a player and asked, "Who's that?" I said, "That's the end." She said, "That's right," and turned it off.

— Robert Orben

When I went to Catholic High School in Philadelphia, we just had one coach for football and basketball. He took all of us who turned out and had us run through the forest. The ones who ran into the trees were on the football team.

— George Raveling

They were all home games and I never had to worry about the alumni.

— Homer Rice, on why being the coach of a prison team was his best job

I won't know until my barber tells me on Monday.

— Knute Rockne, on why Notre Dame lost

How to tackle.

— Cliff Stoudt, on what he learned after throwing three interceptions in a game

It has been my experience that the fastest man on the football field is the quarterback who has just had his pass intercepted.

— Barry Switzer

It's amazing what the human body can do when chased by a bigger human body.

— Jack Thompson

Football features two of the worst aspects of American life – violence and committee meetings.

— *George Will*

Forecasts

There are many methods for predicting the future. For example, you can read horoscopes, tea leaves, tarot cards or crystal balls. Collectively, these methods are known as nutty methods. Or you can put well-researched facts into sophisticated computer models, more commonly referred to as a complete waste of time.

— *Scott Adams*

No matter what happens, there is someone who knew it would.

— *Anonymous*

Anyone who says businessmen deal in facts, not fiction, has never read old five-year projections.

— *Malcolm Forbes*

There are two sorts of forecasters. Those who don't know and those who don't know they don't know.

— *John Kenneth Galbraith*

Friends

Platonic friendship: One that half the town says isn't.

— *Anonymous*

Friendship: Two women mad at the same person.

— *Anonymous*

Old college classmate: Someone who's gotten so bald and fat that he sees you at a class reunion and doesn't recognize you.

— *Anonymous*

Money won't buy friendship, but a set of jumper cables will.

— *Anonymous*

You never know how many friends you have until you rent a cottage at the beach.

— *Kraig Kristofferson*

She's my best friend. She thinks I'm too thin, and I think she's a natural blond.

— *Carrie Snow*

The holy passion of friendship is so sweet and steady and loyal and enduring in nature that it will last through a whole lifetime, if not asked to lend money.

— *Mark Twain*

Frugal

My mother won't admit it, but I've always been a disappointment to her. Deep down inside, she'll never forgive herself for giving birth to a daughter who refuses to launder aluminum foil and use it over again.

— *Erma Bombeck*

Fun

Who needs Disney World? My kids get as much of a thrill when we drive the car through the car wash.

— *Oliver Coe*

Furniture

We sell unfinished furniture.

— *Sign in Christmas tree lot the day after Christmas*

The only really good place to buy lumber is at a store where the lumber has already been cut and attached together in the form of furniture, finished and put inside boxes.

— *Dave Barry*

Early relative – things my relatives gave me.

— *Shelley Winters, on how her house was furnished*

Futons

Futon is a Japanese word that means "sore back."

— *Nick Arnette*

Gadgets

Gadget: Any mechanical device that performs a kitchen task in one-twentieth the time it takes to find it.

— *Anonymous*

Always be wary of any helpful item that weights less than its operating manual.

— *Terry Pratchett*

Gambling

The most common statement made by husbands to wives in Las Vegas: "Give me the money I told you not to give me."

— *Anonymous*

I went to the racetrack today but it was shut, so I just pushed all my money through the gate.

— *W.C. Fields*

It always bothers me to put a silver dollar in a slot machine and then pull the handle down. It's the same motion you use to flush.

— *Robert Orben*

A casino is a place where you lose a hundred dollars in a slot machine and shrug your shoulders, then lose one dollar in a Coke machine and swear like crazy.

— *Jeff Shaw*

Garages

My wife backed out of the garage this morning, but she forgot she backed in last night.

— *Anonymous*

Few things have a shorter life span than a clean garage.

— *Anonymous*

Gardens

The chief objection to gardening is that by the time your back gets used to it, your enthusiasm is gone.

— *Anonymous*

As a gardener, your first job is to prepare the soil. The best tool for this is your neighbor's motorized garden tiller. If your neighbor does not own a garden tiller, suggest that he buy one.

— *Dave Barry*

If you water it and it dies, it's a plant. If you pull it out and it grows back, it's a weed.

— *Gallagher*

My father was never the type to putter around the house on weekends fixing things, mowing the lawn or tending to garden beds. When my younger sister first learned from our mother that babies were made "when Daddy planted a seed in Mommy," she shot back, "That's IMPOSSIBLE. Daddy has never planted a single seed in his entire life!"

— *Susan Harper*

Perennials are the ones that grow like weeds, biennials are the ones that die this year instead of next and hardy annuals are the ones that never come up at all.

— *Katherine Whitehorn*

Gas
Gas: Something your son can somehow manage to drive the family car into the garage on the last drop of.

— *Anonymous*

Generosity
We'd all like a reputation for generosity, and we'd all like to buy it cheap.
— *Mignon McLaughlin*

Geniuses
A genius is one who can do anything except make a living.

— *Joey Adams*

Genius: A man who is ahead of his time, but behind in his rent.

— *Anonymous*

Every family should have at least three children. Then if one is a genius the other two can support him.

— *George Coote*

In every work of genius we recognize our own rejected thoughts; they come back to us with a certain alienated majesty.

— *Ralph Waldo Emerson*

If children grew up according to early indications, we should have nothing but geniuses.

— *Johann von Goethe*

Sometimes men come by the name of genius in the same way that certain insects come by the name of centipede – not because they have a hundred feet, but because most people can't count above fourteen.

— *George Lightenberg*

Smart is when you only believe half of what you hear. Brilliant is when you know which half.

— *Robert Orben*

Gifted Children
It's a rare parent who can see his or her child clearly and objectively. At a school board meeting I attended, the only definition of a gifted child on which everyone in the audience could agree was "mine."

— *Jane Adams*

Show-off: A child who is more talented than yours.

— *Anonymous*

There must be such a thing as a child with average ability, but you can't find a parent who will admit that it is his child.

— *Thomas Bailey*

Gifts
This year let's give each other more practical gifts like socks and fur coats.
— *Anonymous, wife to husband*

I know, but I didn't think you meant neckties.
— *Anonymous, nephew's response to aunt who asked if he preferred large checks or small checks*

One of the disadvantages of having children is that they eventually get old enough to give you presents they make at school.
— *Robert Byrne*

A word to new brides: if you want to be remembered forever, don't write a thank-you note for a wedding gift.
— *Edward Rankin, Jr.*

I never know what to get my father for his birthday. Once I gave him a hundred dollars and said, "Buy yourself something that will make your life easier." So he went out and bought a present for my mother.
— *Rita Rudner*

Girdles
The pastor would appreciate it if the ladies of the congregation would lend him their electric girdles for the pancake breakfast next Sunday morning.
— *Church bulletin*

Giving
It is better to give than to lend, and it costs about the same.
— *Philip Gibbs*

I try to raise my kids to be generous and sharing. The other day, my three-year-old daughter offered me her bag of sweets and said, "Take a lot. Take two."
— *Edward Price*

Giving Birth
Sign seen on a maternity-ward door: "Push! Push! Push!"
— *Anonymous*

Mrs. James Morse Thirkall
 is pleased to announce
 the arrival of
 Mary Nelly – 6 pounds 8 ounces
 and the loss of twenty pounds

— Anonymous

Hard labor: A redundancy, like *working mother.*

— Joyce Armor

When my wife was giving birth, she tried the breathing exercises and they were really effective for, oh, I'd say fifteen, even twenty, seconds. Then she switched to the more traditional method, which is screaming for drugs.

— Dave Barry

Giving birth is like pushing a piano through a transom.

— Fanny Brice

At the next contraction, my wife told everyone in the delivery room that my parents were never married.

— Bill Cosby

Once you have a kid you'll never win another argument with your wife, because in the game of marriage, giving birth is a royal flush. Nothing trumps motherhood.

— Reno Goodale

Having a baby can be a scream.

— Joan Rivers

I just talked to the doctor. He told me her contraptions were an hour apart.

— Mackey Sasser

Glasses

The first time I went outside with my new trifocals, I took a three-mile walk through the lobby of my ophthalmologist's building, climbed a five-foot curb and then met an autograph seeker who happened to be a giant eyeball. "Mr. Cosby, could I have your autograph?" "Yes, yes! Just don't eat me!"

— Bill Cosby

Right now I can't find my glasses without my glasses.

— *Art Howe*

Glue

Super glue is forever.

— *Anonymous, things I've learned from my children*

I bought a tube of Krazy Glue and the label fell off.

— *Jay Leno*

Gluttons

Glutton: Someone who eats the slice of cake you wanted.

— *Anonymous*

God

A little girl, drawing a picture, was asked by her mother: "What are you drawing?" She replied: "A picture of God!" "But we don't know what God looks like," her mother objected. "Well," replied the child, "when I am finished with this then you will know what God looks like!"

— *Ronald Rolheiser*

I always figured God had eyebrows just like Pop's, and when somebody lied or stole or punched a person in the face, God's eyebrows went right up like Pop's.

— *Cynthia Rylant*

God's Mercy

What a wanton waste of the mercies of God's providence.

— *Benjamin Disraeli, when he saw a deaf Member of Parliament listening to the debate with the aid of an ear trumpet*

Golf

Every club has a swing narcissist, who, on and off the course, constantly practices his swing. I remember *Never-Play Joe* at Chandler Park, who hung around the clubhouse and putting green all day practicing his swing. He usually didn't even have a club in his hands and rarely ever hit a ball, yet he was constantly swinging.

— *Joseph Amato*

The golf pro walked over to two women and asked, "Are you here to learn how to play golf?"

One replied, "My friend is. I learned yesterday."

— *Anonymous*

"Go in! Go in!": A phrase yelled by golfers attempting to sink a difficult putt, or by those playing behind a slow foursome.

— *Anonymous*

Zillion to one: 1) The odds against hitting a hole-in-one. 2) The odds in favor of hitting a two-inch diameter tree that is 170 yards away.

— *Anonymous*

My wife said, "You're so wrapped up in golf you don't even remember our wedding day!"

"Sure I do," I said. "That's the day I sank that thirty-foot putt!"

— *Anonymous*

He has a swing like an octopus falling out of a tree.

— *Anonymous*

Lost: Golfing husband and dog – last seen at Ratliff Ranch Golf Links. Reward for dog.

— *Anonymous*

I sank a long and curling putt,
  It's like I've seldom seen;
  It would have helped my scoring but,
  'Twas on the practice green.

— *Richard Armour*

The less skilled the player, the more likely he is to share his ideas about the golf swing.

— *Henry Beard*

Tap-in: A putt short enough to be missed one-handed.

— *Henry Beard*

A golf ball will always travel furthest when hit in the wrong direction.

— *Henry Beard*

It's often necessary to hit a second shot to really appreciate the first one.

— *Henry Beard*

If swinging the club really was as simple and natural as, say, swinging a hammer, Corey Pavin would be making $8.47 an hour.

— *Henry Beard*

A golf match is a test of your skill against your opponent's luck.

— *Henry Beard*

The shortest distance between any two points on a golf course is a straight line that passes directly through the center of a very large tree.

— *Henry Beard*

A golf ball will always come to rest halfway down a hill, unless there is sand or water at the bottom.

— *Henry Beard*

On courses where the yardages are marked on sprinkler heads: 1) There will be no sprinkler head within forty yards of your ball. 2) The nearest sprinkler head will be blank. 3) While being examined, the sprinkler head will turn on.

— *Henry Beard*

It's amazing how many people beat you at golf once you're no longer president.

— *George Bush*

Duffer's Laws: 1) The best way for a Duffer to go around a tree standing directly in his line is to aim directly at the tree, since you never hit where you aim anyway. 2) The only time you'll ever hit the ball straight is when you're applying Duffer's Law number one.

— *John Corcoran*

Tree: Hostile, agile growth that jumps out of your opponent's way.

— *Paul Dickson*

The golf swing is among the most stressful and unnatural acts in sports, short of cheering for the Yankees.

— Brad Faxon

Jim Furyk has a swing like a man trying to kill a snake in a phone booth.

— David Feherty

Bisque: An agreed-to extra shot.
    Bisquick: Rapid extra unagreed-upon shot taken before others notice.

— Bill Geist

Golf and women are a lot alike. You know you are not going to wind up with anything but grief, but you can't resist the impulse.

— Jackie Gleason

The reason for playing golf? To turn your boredom into frustration.

— Buddy Hackett

When your car was stolen you said your golf clubs were in the trunk. You failed to mention your wife was in the front seat.

— David Harbough

Bing Crosby was an excellent player, with the slowest backswing I've ever seen. While he was taking the club back you could fit him for a tailored suit.

— Bob Hope

[Based on the old adage that "space occupied by a given tree is ten percent wood and ninety percent air."] A golf ball driven through the branches of a tree will hit the ten-percent wood ninety percent of the time, and the ninety-percent air ten percent of the time.

— R.D. Johnson

I don't know. I've never played there.

— Sandy Lyle, on his opinion of the then promising amateur, Tiger Woods

In a large locker room, with hundreds of lockers, the few people using the facility at any one time will all be at their lockers and will be next to each other so that everybody is cramped.

— *Gary Neustadter*

If mastering the golf swing is really nothing more than a matter of developing the muscle memory necessary to perform an unfamiliar physical movement like, say, riding a bicycle, then why aren't there 7,500 books on how to ride a bicycle.

— *Leslie Nielson*

Anytime you get the urge to golf, instead take eighteen minutes and beat your head against a good solid wall. This is guaranteed to duplicate to a tee the physical and emotional beating you would have suffered playing a round of golf.

— *Mark Oman*

There are times when I find myself wishing that my wife would learn to like golf – not to the point of taking it up herself, of course, but perhaps to the point of joining me some afternoon for a few happy hours spent watching videotapes of my swing.

— *David Owen*

A pretty girl will always have the toughest time learning to play golf, because every man wants to give her lessons.

— *Harvey Penick*

I have played a lot of golf with preachers. One minister I recall would, after missing a short putt, turn to another member of the group and ask, "Would you mind expressing my sentiments about that?"

— *Harvey Penick*

The other day I was playing golf and saw an unusual thing. A golfer became so mad that he threw his brand-new set of golf clubs into the lake. A few minutes later he came back, waded into the lake, and retrieved his clubs. He proceeded to take his car keys out of the bag and then threw the clubs back into the water.

— *Bob Phillips*

Promising golfer: Any younger player who listens attentively to your advice and nods his head in agreement.

— *Martin Ragaway*

Long game: Shots where considerable distance is important. A match you are hopelessly losing is a very long game.

— *Martin Ragaway*

Golf is good for the soul. You get so mad at yourself you forget to hate your enemies.

— *Will Rogers*

My swing is so bad I look like a caveman killing his lunch.

— *Lee Trevino*

My golf swing is a bit like ironing a shirt. You get one side smoothed out, turn it over and there is a big wrinkle on the other side. Then you iron that one out, turn it over and there is yet another wrinkle.

— *Tom Watson*

I am not happy with my golf game. Maybe I should read my own book.

— *Ian Woosnam*

Honey, do you have anything to say before the golf season starts?

— *Robert Zorn*

Golf Balls
Brand new golf balls are water-magnetic.

— *Anonymous*

For most golfers, the only difference between a one-dollar ball and a three-dollar ball is two dollars.

— *Henry Beard*

In early spring, when the course is too wet to walk on, some winter golfers I know prowl the edges of the fairways, looking for old balls that have popped up through the thawing ground like corpses of gangsters rising in the Hudson River.

— *David Owen*

The centers of golf balls are wrapped in rubber bands, almost as tensely as most golfers who try to hit them.

— *Arnold Palmer*

Golf Clubs

The best way to cause the prompt reappearance of a club lost on the course is to order a replacement.

— *Henry Beard*

My car absolutely will not run unless my golf clubs are in the trunk.

— *Bruce Berlet*

Some people rent clubs until they're sure the game of golf agrees with them. For a real bargain, you can often wait around the eighteenth green and pick up a set cheap from a guy who is just giving up the game.

— *Joe James*

There are many ways to punish a putter, such as burning, rusting and drowning, but the most tortuous is to drag it along the pavement out of the door of a fast-moving vehicle.

— *Dan Jenkins*

In my house in Houston I still have that putter with which I missed that two-and-a-half-foot putt to win the Open. It's in two places.

— *Doug Sanders*

Good Old Days

Nothing is more responsible for the good old days than a bad memory.

— *Franklin Adams*

If you're yearning for the good old days, just turn off the air-conditioning.

— *Griff Niblack*

Gossip

Nothing makes a long story short like the arrival of the person you were talking about.

— *Anonymous*

I won't go into all the details, dear. In fact, I've already told you more about it than I heard myself.

— *Anonymous*

When a bunch of girls get together, the Lord pity the first one who leaves.

— *Anonymous*

Don't talk about yourself. It'll be done when you leave.

— *Anonymous*

There isn't much to be seen in a little town, but what you hear can make up for it.

— *Kin Hubbard*

Of course I wouldn't say anything about her unless I could say something good. And, oh boy, is this good . . .

— *Bill King*

A gossip is one who talks to you about others, a bore is one who talks to you about himself, and a brilliant conversationalist is one who talks to you about yourself.

— *Lisa Kirk*

If you can't say anything good about someone, sit right here by me.

— *Alice Longworth*

Every office has gossip. If you never hear any, you're it.

— *Gene Perret*

Conversation is when three women stand on the corner talking. *Gossip* is when one of them leaves.

— *Herb Shriner*

Hear no evil, speak no evil – and you'll never be invited to a party.

— *Oscar Wilde*

Government

We understand there are millions in the budget for emergencies which we can develop in a hurry if necessary.

— Anonymous

Congress, after years of stalling, finally got around to clearing the way for informal discussions that might lead to possible formal talks that could potentially produce some kind of tentative agreements . . .

— Dave Barry

Too bad the only people who know how to run the country are busy driving cabs and cutting hair.

— George Burns

You spend a billion here and a billion there. Sooner or later, it adds up to real money.

— Everett Dirksen, Illinois Senator

We may not imagine how our lives could be more frustrating and complex – but Congress can.

— Joe Griffith

Talk is cheap – except when Congress does it.

— Cullen Hightower

The mistakes made by Congress wouldn't be so bad if the next Congress didn't keep trying to correct them.

— Cullen Hightower

It's a terribly hard job to spend a billion dollars and get your money's worth.
— George Humphrey, former secretary of the Treasury

The supply of government exceeds the demand.

— Lewis Lapham

It's fine with me if the undertaker doesn't mind.
— Abraham Lincoln, to a persistent caller who came to him with the news that the chief of customs had just died, and asked if he could take his place

Isn't there something we can appear to be doing?

> — *Henry Cabot Lodge, in a letter to Theodore Roosevelt during the 1902 coal strike*

A penny saved is a Congressional oversight.

> — *Hal Lee Luyah*

No matter what your religion, you should try to become a government program, for then you will have everlasting life.

> — *Lynn Martin, U.S. Representative*

The only thing that saves us from the bureaucracy is its inefficiency.

> — *Eugene McCarthy*

If your business is going to hell, big government is often the travel agent.

> — *Robert Orben*

If you think health care is expensive now, wait until you see what it costs when it's free.

> — *P.J. O'Rourke*

Sloths move at the speed of congressional debate but with greater deliberation and less noise.

> — *P.J. O'Rourke*

Democracy is a process by which the people are free to choose the man who will get the blame.

> — *Laurence Peter*

The most delicious of all privileges – spending other people's money.

> — *John Randolph, on serving in Congress*

Government programs, once launched, never disappear. Actually, a government bureau is the nearest thing to eternal life we'll ever see on earth.

> — *Ronald Reagan*

I have left orders to be awakened at any time in case of national emergency, even if I'm in a cabinet meeting.

> — *Ronald Reagan*

Did you hear that the communists now have a million-dollar lottery for their people? The winners get a dollar a year for a million years.

— *Ronald Reagan*

Government's view of the economy could be summed up in a few short phrases: if it moves, tax it; if it keeps moving, regulate it; and if it stops moving, subsidize it.

— *Ronald Reagan*

One way to make sure crime doesn't pay would be to let the government run it.

— *Ronald Reagan*

Government does not solve problems – it subsidizes them.

— *Ronald Reagan*

Thank heaven we don't get all the government we pay for.

— *Will Rogers*

I see a committee that was investigating the high cost of living, turned in their report: "We find the cost of living very high and we recommend more funds to carry on the investigation."

— *Will Rogers*

Mr. Coolidge is the best Democrat we ever had in the White House. He didn't do nothin', but that's what we wanted done.

— *Will Rogers*

There is good news from Washington today. Congress is deadlocked and can't act.

— *Will Rogers*

Alexander Hamilton started the U.S. Treasury with nothing – and that was the closest our country has ever been to being even.

— *Will Rogers*

Congress is so strange. A man gets up to speak and says nothing. Nobody listens. And then everybody disagrees.

— *Will Rogers*

Great Funny Quotes

The Treasury department has saved some money, but it showed that it cost fifty million more to save it than it did the same department last year, showing that even the cost of saving money has gone up.

— *Will Rogers*

A government which robs Peter to pay Paul can always depend on the support of Paul.

— *George Bernard Shaw*

If you don't know one of these new fellas, just call him Mr. Chairman and you're safe.
— *Morris Udal, on all the congressional committees and subcommittees that have been created over the years*

There are blessed intervals when I forget by one means or another that I am president of the Unites States.

— *Woodrow Wilson*

Grandparents

Grandparents: The people who think your children are wonderful even though they're sure you're not raising them right.

— *Anonymous*

You feel completely comfortable entrusting your baby to them for long periods, which is why most grandparents flee to Florida at the earliest opportunity.

— *Dave Barry*

If your baby is beautiful and perfect, never cries or fusses, sleeps on schedule and burps on demand, an angel all the time – you're the grandma.

— *Teresa Bloomingdale*

When we grandchildren were all gathered around the dinner table bored out of our minds, when no other adult was watching, eyes twinkling my grandmother would quietly detach her upper bridge and roll it out on her tongue with three tiny false teeth riding on it, and as our eyes bugged out, we could hear her characteristic deep delighted chuckle.

— *Susan Kenney*

A mother becomes a true grandmother the day she stops noticing the terrible things her children do because she is so enchanted with the wonderful things her grandchildren do.

— *Lois Wyse*

Grass
All you need to grow fine, vigorous grass is a crack in your sidewalk.

— *Anonymous*

Guests
All our guests bring us happiness – some in coming, some in going.

— *Anonymous*

It's what the guests say as they swing out of the driveway that really counts.

— *Anonymous*

A husband's job is to keep talking to unexpected guests at the front gate while his wife straightens out the living room.

— *Anonymous*

The two biggest liars in the world: the guest who keeps saying, "I must be going" and the host who asks, "What's your hurry?"

— *Anonymous*

Easy come, easy go, does not apply to houseguests.

— *Leo Rosten*

The art of hospitality is to make guests feel at home when you wish they were.

— *Violet Smart*

Introduce yourselves; I can smell something burning.
  — *Katherine Whitehorn, recommended greeting for hostesses who have forgotten guests' names*

Guilt
He looked like a man who's just realized that he's posted a love letter in the wrong envelope.

— *Hugh Laurie*

Habits

Nothing so needs reforming as other people's habits.

— Mark Twain

To cease smoking is the easiest thing. I ought to know. I've done it a thousand times.

— Mark Twain

Hair

Trouble turns a man's hair gray in one night. Vanity turns a woman's hair any color in one minute.

— Anonymous

The girl had long black hair and wore long black gloves to cover it.

— Anonymous

Tom sees Harry on the street and shouts, "What did you do to your hair? It looks like a wig!"

Harry looks embarrassed and says, "Well, it is a wig."

Tom replies, "You know what, you'd never be able to tell."

— Anonymous

Life is an endless struggle full of frustrations and challenges but eventually you find a hairstylist you like.

— Anonymous

A toupee is a nest that sets on the egg.

— Arthur "Bugs" Baer

Dad, who was the finest human being I have ever known, but who had the hairstyling skills and fashion flair of a lathe operator – cut my hair. This meant that I spent my critical junior high school years underneath what looked like the pelt of some very sick rodent.

— Dave Barry

Just once I would like to run and feel the wind in my hair.

— Rocky Bleier, imagining what it would be like to have hair

It's great to have gray hair. Ask anyone who's bald.

— *Rodney Dangerfield*

It's an ill wind that blows when you leave the hairdresser.

— *Phyllis Diller*

The first time I saw Dick Vitale, his hair was blowing in the breeze. And he was too proud to chase it.

— *Cliff Ellis*

My days of having hair are numbered. The once-bustling downtown of my abundantly populated scalp is becoming a wasteland of burned-out storefronts and boarded-up windows as the occupants move to the outly-ing suburbs of my neck, ears and back.

— *Dennis Miller*

There are certain telltale signs that you might be losing your hair that you should be aware of . . . . If you notice your barber just making the clicking noise with the scissors without actually touching your hair.

— *Dennis Miller*

I'm not offended by dumb blonde jokes because I know that I'm not dumb. I also know that I'm not blonde.

— *Dolly Parton*

Have you ever had one of those nights when you didn't want to go out but your hair looked too good to stay home?

— *Jack Simmons*

When redheaded people are above a certain social grade, their hair is auburn.

— *Mark Twain*

Happiness

Happiness is having a large, loving, caring, close-knit family in another city.

— *George Burns*

Harpists

Harpists spend ninety percent of their lives tuning their harps and ten percent playing out of tune.

— *Igor Stravinsky*

Harpsichords

The sound of the harpsichord resembles that of a bird-cage played with toasting-forks.

— *Thomas Beecham*

Hats

Pat: "Whenever I'm down in the dumps, I get myself another hat."
  Sue: "I wondered where you found them."

— *Anonymous*

When I was six I made my mother a little hat – out of her new blouse.

— *Lilly Daché*

When a man buys a new hat, he wants one just like the one he had before. But a woman isn't that way.

— *Edgar Howe*

Someone you like is wearing an ugly hat, and she asks you to give her your honest opinion of it: "What a lovely chapeau! But if I may make one teensy suggestion? If it blows off, don't chase it."

— *Miss Piggy*

Headlines

The best headlines never fi

— *Bernard Levin*

Health

He went for his annual physical. After the examination, the doctor said to his wife, "I don't like the looks of him." The wife said, "I don't either, but he's so good to the kids."

— *Anonymous*

Minor surgery is surgery someone else is having.

— *Joseph Cook*

Nobody is sicker than the man who is sick on his day off.

— *Bob Phillips*

Heaven

Lutherans believe you cannot get into heaven unless you bring a covered dish.

— *Garrison Keillor*

Hell

Hell, for garage mechanics, will be a land of abundant grease and no steering wheels to wipe it on.

— *Anonymous*

DO YOU KNOW
WHAT HELL IS LIKE?
COME IN AND HEAR
OUR CHOIR.

— *Sign outside a church*

Hell: Home of the most magnificent golf course you've ever seen, complete with top line pro clubs, all gratis. But not a single golf ball.

— *Martin Ragaway*

Help From Others

When somebody does something for your own good, you can be sure you won't like it.

— *Anonymous*

Heredity

There is absolutely nothing that confirms one's belief in heredity more than having a handsome child.

— *Anonymous*

Heredity is what a man believes in until his son begins to behave like a delinquent.

— *Anonymous*

All good qualities in a child are the result of environment, while all the bad ones are the result of poor heredity on the side of the other parent.

— *Elinor Smith*

High School

It is hard to convince a high school student that he will encounter a lot of problems more difficult than those of algebra and geometry.

— *Edgar Howe*

A high school in Connecticut has a power-nap club. We called that algebra class.

— *Jay Leno*

High-Tech

The trouble with high-tech is that you always end up using scissors.

— *David Hockney*

Hockey

A puck is a hard rubber disc that hockey players strike when they can't hit one another.

— *Jimmy Cannon*

Geez, I hate to waste my goal in a practice game.

— *Craig Ludwig, on scoring in an exhibition game after scoring only six goals in five seasons*

Half the game is mental; the other half is being mental.

— *Jim McKenny, on hockey*

Goaltending is a normal job. Sure! How would you like it in your job if every time you made a small mistake, a red light went on over your desk and fifteen thousand people stood up and yelled at you?

— *Jacques Plante*

Hockey belongs to the Cartoon Network, where a person can be pancaked by an ACME anvil, then expanded – accordion-style – back to full stature, without any lasting side effect.

— *Steve Ruskin*

It's like going out with the best-looking girl in high school. You know she's going to dump you eventually. But still, you've got to go for it.
— *Gord Stellick, on being the Maple Leafs' general manager under Harold Ballard*

The only job worse is a javelin catcher at a track-and-field meet.
— *Gump Worsley, on goaltending*

Hole-in-one
Pity the man who told his boss he was going to a funeral but instead went to the golf course and shot his first hole-in-one.
— *Anonymous*

Hole-in-one: A ball hit directly from the tee into the hole on a single shot by a golfer playing alone.
— *Henry Beard and Roy McKie*

Man blames fate for other accidents but feels personally responsible for a hole-in-one.
— *Martha Beckman*

You can always spot an employee who's playing golf with his boss. He's the fellow who gets a hole-in-one and says, "Oops!"
— *Bob Monkhouse*

Holes
Follow the first law of holes: If you are in one, stop digging.
— *Dennis Healey*

Holidays
Thanksgiving dinners take eighteen hours to prepare. They are consumed in twelve minutes. Half-times take twelve minutes. This is not a coincidence.
— *Erma Bombeck*

Labor Day is a glorious holiday because your child will be going back to school the next day. It would have been called Independence Day, but that name was already taken.
— *Bill Dodds*

If all the cars in the United States were placed end to end, it would probably be Labor Day Weekend.

— *Doug Larson*

Home

There isn't a child who hasn't gone out into the brave new world who eventually doesn't return to the old homestead carrying a bundle of dirty clothes.

— *Art Buchwald*

Thomas Wolfe wrote, "You can't go home again." You can, but you'll get treated like an eight-year-old.

— *Daryl Hogue*

Home Improvement

No one can make you feel more humble than the repairman who discovers you've been trying to fix it yourself.

— *Anonymous*

My dad, he'd try anything – carpentry, electrical wiring, plumbing, roofing. From watching him, I learned a lesson that still applies to my life today: No matter how difficult a task may seem, if you're not afraid to try it, you can do it. And when you're done, it will leak.

— *Dave Barry*

Caulking guns are designed so that as soon as you pick them up, the caulking starts oozing out, and it keeps oozing out until there is none left. This is a clever ploy of the caulking manufacturers to keep themselves in business.

— *Dave Barry*

Energy experts tell us that caulking doors and windows is one of the easiest ways to get caulking all over yourself.

— *Dave Barry*

If you want an accurate picture of the time it will take to install something, you need to use a different formula altogether: Calculate the worst-case-scenario amount of time you would be willing to spend on this project, then multiply by four.

— *Karen Linamen*

Homework
When a teenager is watching television, listening to her CD player and talking on the phone, she is probably doing her homework.

— *Anonymous*

Almost every child would learn to write sooner if allowed to do his homework in wet cement.

— *Anonymous*

Adult education will continue as long as kids have homework.

— *Anonymous*

It's a myth that you will be able to help your children with their homework. I'm taking remedial math so I can help my son make it to the third grade.

— *Sinbad*

Honesty
Parents always want their children to tell the truth, the whole truth and nothing but the truth – unless there are visitors present.

— *Anonymous*

Horses
There's nothing like your first horseback ride to make you feel better off.

— *Anonymous*

There are no handles to a horse, but the 1910 model has a string to each side of its face for turning its head when there is something you want it to see.

— *Stephen Leacock*

Hospitals
I just got the bill for my operation. Now I know why those guys wear masks.

— *Jim Boren*

That should assure us of at least 45 minutes of undisturbed privacy.
— *Dorothy Parker, pressing a button marked "Nurse" during a stay in the hospital*

Hotels

It's impossible to sleep in a hotel. Just try to close those curtains. That must be a big joke with the contractors. All of them leave that one-inch slit down the middle. No matter where you lie, the light finds you.
— *Louie Anderson*

A hotel is a place that keeps the manufacturers of 25-watt bulbs in business.
— *Shelley Berman*

I rang the bell of this small bed-and-breakfast place, whereupon a lady appeared at a window. "What do you want?" she asked. I want to stay here," I replied. "Well, stay there then," she said and closed the window.
— *Chic Murray*

He once got back to the hotel after a night on the town and he called the front desk and asked for a 7:00 a.m. wake-up call. The operator said, "You just missed it."
— *Vin Scully, on infielder Gene Freese*

Houses

The dining room is the place where the family eats while the kitchen is being painted.
— *Anonymous*

A good architect can improve the look of an old house merely by discussing the cost of a new one.
— *Anonymous*

Home is the place where, no matter where you're sitting, you're looking at something you should be doing.
— *Anonymous*

Whenever there is a flat surface, someone will find something to put on it.
— *Ballweg*

In any electrical circuit, appliances and wiring will burn out to protect fuses.

— *Robert Byrne*

A builder's estimate is a sum of money equal to half the final cost.

— *Neil Collins*

My mother was an authority on pigsties. "This is the worst-looking pigsty I have ever seen in my life, and I want it cleaned up right now."

— *Bill Cosby*

If your house is really a mess and a stranger comes to the door, greet them with, "Who could have done this? We have no enemies."

— *Phyllis Diller*

Remember – a developer is someone who wants to build a house in the woods. An environmentalist is someone who already owns a house in the woods.

— *Dennis Miller*

We've just moved into our dream house. It costs twice as much as we ever dreamed it would.

— *Bob Phillips*

The easiest way to find something lost around the house is to buy a replacement.

— *Rosenbaum*

When we were finishing our house, we found we had a little cash left over, on account of the plumber not knowing it.

— *Mark Twain*

Housework
Housework is something you do that nobody notices unless you don't do it.

— *Anonymous*

Housework is a treadmill from futility to oblivion with stop-offs at tedium and counter-productivity.

— *Erma Bombeck*

Housework expands to fill the time available plus half an hour.

— *Shirley Conran*

You make the beds, you do the dishes and six months later you have to start all over again.

— *Joan Rivers*

Human Nature

Human nature: Something that makes you swear at a pedestrian when you are driving and at the driver when you are a pedestrian.

— *Anonymous*

Humility

People seldom speak ill of themselves, but when they have a good chance of being contradicted.

— *Fulke Greville*

The trouble with true humility is, you can't talk about it.

— *Michael Thomsett*

If only I had a little more humility, I would be perfect.

— *Ted Turner*

I was humble for a few weeks, but nobody noticed.

— *Katherine Whitehorn*

Husbands

Husbands were made to be talked to. It helps them concentrate on what they're reading.

— *Anonymous*

Husband: A curious mammal who buys his football tickets in June and his wife's Christmas present on December 24.

— *Anonymous*

A smart husband buys his wife fine china so she won't trust him to wash it.

— *Anonymous*

The best way to get most husbands to do something is to suggest that perhaps they're too old to do it.

— *Shirley MacLaine*

My husband forgot my birthday and my anniversary. I didn't feel bad. On the contrary. Give me a guilty husband any day. Some of my best outfits come from his guilt.

— *Betty Walker*

People are either hunting for husbands or hiding from them.

— *Oscar Wilde*

Ideas

Exhilaration is that feeling you get just after a great idea hits you but before you realize what's wrong with it.

— *Anonymous*

The idea is interesting and well-formed, but in order to earn better than a C, the idea must be feasible.

— *Yale management professor to Federal Express Founder Fred Smith on his paper proposing reliable overnight delivery service*

It's like the beaver told the rabbit as they stared up at the immense wall of Hoover Dam, "No, I didn't actually build it myself. But it was based on an idea of mine."

— *Charles Townes*

Ignorance

Ignorance is strange. It picks up confidence as it goes along.

— *Anonymous*

Illegibility

Illegibility: A doctor's prescription written with a post office pen in the rumble seat of an antique car.

— *Anonymous*

Imagination

Peter could have been setting his school on fire or feeding his sister to an alligator and escaping in a hot-air balloon, but all grown-ups saw was a boy staring at the blue sky without blinking, a boy who did not hear you when you called his name.

— *Ian McEwan*

Imagination is something that sits up with Dad and Mom the first time their teenager stays out late.

— *Lane Olinghouse*

Skill without imagination is craftsmanship and gives us many useful objects such as wickerwork picnic baskets. Imagination without skill gives us modern art.

— *Tom Stoppard*

Impatience

This deep-fat fryer can flash-fry a buffalo in under forty seconds.
    Forty seconds? But I want it now!

— *Homer Simpson,* The Simpsons

Impossible

There are only two things that are really impossible: putting toothpaste back in the tube and getting off a mailing list.

— *Anonymous*

A person who says nothing is impossible has never tried to remove bubble gum from an angora sweater.

— *Anonymous*

The only problem with doing the impossible is that everybody expects you to duplicate it.

— *John McKay*

Indecision

Indecision may or may not be my problem.

— *Jimmy Buffett*

I'll give you a definite maybe.

— *Samuel Goldwyn*

I had one boss who loved decision making. He'd make several decisions on the same problem five, six, seven times a day.

— *Gene Perret*

Inflation
Inflation: What used to cost twenty dollars to buy now costs forty dollars to repair.

— *Anonymous*

Influence
Any time you think you have influence, try ordering around someone else's dog.

— *Anonymous*

Injuries
Taylor, we've run out of time outs. Go in there and get hurt.

— *George Halas*

The hardest thing about prize fightin' is pickin' up yer teeth with a boxing glove on.

— *Kin Hubbard*

I now judge all illnesses and injuries solely according to their probable impact on my game.

— *David Owen*

I used to think that if I suffered some terrible injury to my hands, I would have the surgeon fuse my fingers so that they would fit on the home keys of a typewriter keyboard; I now know that I would have them fused in a slightly strong overlapping golf grip.

— *David Owen*

Insect Repellent
Insect repellent: One of a number of *gag* items available in the novelty sections of tackle shops, along with *waterproof* clothing, *damp-proof* matches and *long-life* batteries.

— *Henry Beard and Roy McKie*

Insomnia

Insomnia: A contagious disease often transmitted from babies to parents.

— *Shannon Fife*

Inspiration

The ultimate inspiration is the deadline.

— *Nolan Bushnell*

Instructions

Clearly stated instructions will produce multiple interpretations.

— *Anonymous*

Insurance

The insurance salesman said to me, "Don't let me frighten you into a hasty decision. Sleep on it tonight. If you wake up tomorrow, let me know."

— *Anonymous*

The insurance man told me that the accident policy covered falling off the roof but not hitting the ground.

— *Tommy Cooper*

Integrity

When a man says his word is as good as his bond, always take his bond.

— *Hugo Vickers*

Intelligence

Intellectual: A guy who can keep his mind on a book at a beach.

— *Anonymous*

I'm in a phone booth at the corner of Walk and Don't Walk.

— *Anonymous*

I'm not as smart as I used to be. But you can't stay a teenager all of your life.

— *Anonymous*

An intellectual is a man who takes more words than he needs to say more than he knows.

— *Dwight D. Eisenhower*

Genius has limits; stupidity does not.

— Elbert Hubbard

Intelligence is like four-wheel drive. It only allows you to get stuck in more remote places.

— Garrison Keillor

I seldom said anything smart when I was a child. I tried it once or twice, but it was not popular.

— Mark Twain

If you don't think too good, don't think too much.

— Ted Williams

Internet
Getting information from the Internet is like trying to get a glass of water from Niagara Falls.

— Arthur Clarke

Intuition
Intuition: The strange instinct that tells a woman she's right, whether she is or not.

— Oscar Wilde

Inventions
Everything that can be invented has been invented.

— Charles Duell, Commissioner, U.S. Office of Patents, 1899

Will you quit worrying about better ways to light the house and go get me some stove wood.

— Nancy Edison, to her son Thomas

If Thomas Edison had gone to business school, we would all be reading by larger candles.

— Mark McCormack

Investments
It never freezes in Florida, at least not until you buy an orange grove.

— Anonymous

Many men who refuse to believe in Santa Clause are convinced they can beat Wall Street.

— *Anonymous*

One of the funny things about the stock market is that every time one man buys, another sells, and both think they are astute.

— *William Feather*

I've been studying all the economic forecasts and have come to the conclusion that the best time to buy anything is when I don't have any money.

— *David Griffith*

A thousand dollars invested at just eight percent for 400 years grows to $23 quadrillion. But the first 100 years are the hardest.

— *Sidney Homer*

I could go out and buy 200,000 acres of timberland, but then what would I do? Cheer for the trees?

— *David McConnell, New York millionaire, on why he was interested in purchasing an NFL franchise*

Gentlemen prefer bonds.

— *Andrew Mellon*

There are only two times in a man's life when he should not speculate; when he can't afford it, and when he can.

— *Mark Twain*

October is one of the peculiarly dangerous months to speculate in stocks. The others are July, January, September, April, November, May, March, June, December, August and February.

— *Mark Twain*

Ironing
My second favorite household chore is ironing. My first is hitting my head on the top bunk bed until I faint.

— *Erma Bombeck*

I just don't buy temporary insanity as a murder defense. Breaking into someone's home and ironing all their clothes – that's temporary insanity.

— *Sue Kolinsky*

Irritation

Everything you do irritates me. And when you're not here, the things I know you're gonna do when you come back in irritate me.

— *Neil Simon*

Italics

Italics: The language spoken by ancient Italians.

— *Anonymous, definition by a child*

Jelly

Jelly is a food commonly found on kids, bread and piano keys.

— *Anonymous*

Job Interviews

At a job interview, tell them you're willing to give 110 percent – unless the job is statistician.

— *Adam Gropman*

Robinson's Law: The guy you beat out of a prime parking space is the one you have to see for a job interview.

— *Cal Robinson*

Jogging

My doctor recently told me that jogging could add years to my life. I think he was right. I feel ten years older already.

— *Milton Berle*

The trouble with jogging is that by the time you realize you've not in shape for it, it's too far to walk back.

— *Franklin Jones*

The first time I see a jogger smiling, I'll consider it.

— *Joan Rivers*

Journalism

I daren't take a holiday. If I stop writing my column for a month it might affect the circulation of the newspaper – or it might not.

— Arthur Brisbane

Sometimes the media writes what I say and not what I mean.

— Pedro Guerrero

June Bugs

I've learned that when you put a June bug down a girl's dress, she goes crazy.

— Anonymous, age six

Junk

Junk is something you throw away three weeks before you need it.

— Anonymous

The only difference between a yard sale and a trash pickup is how close to the road the stuff is placed.

— Anonymous

Juvenile Delinquency

Juvenile delinquency: The result of parents trying to train children without starting at the bottom.

— Anonymous

Karate

Karate is a form of martial arts in which people who have had years and years of training can, using only their hands and feet, make some of the worst movies in the history of the world.

— Dave Barry

Kickbacks

A kickback is where the giver says, "Thank you," and the recipient says, "Don't mention it."

— Robert Orben

Kissing

"Would you call for help if I tried to kiss you?"
    "Do you need help?"

— *Anonymous*

It might help to watch soap operas all day.
        — *Carin, age nine, when asked how a person learns to kiss*

It's never okay to kiss a boy. They always slobber all over you. That's why I stopped doing it.
        — *Jean, age ten, when asked when it's okay to kiss someone*

I wasn't kissing her, I was whispering in her mouth.
                            — *Chico Marx*

He kissed her once by the pigsty when she wasn't looking and never kissed her again although she was looking all the time.
                            — *Dylan Thomas*

Kissing is a means of getting two people so close together that they can't see anything wrong with each other.
                            — *René Yasenek*

Knowledge

I've learned one thing – people who know the least seem to know it the loudest.

— *Andy Capp*

Land

A man complained that on his way home to dinner he had every day to pass through that long field of his neighbor's. I advised him to buy it, and it would never seem long again.
                    — *Ralph Waldo Emerson*

Laughter

I am thankful for laughter, except when milk comes out of my nose.
                            — *Woody Allen*

She laughs at everything you say. Why? Because she has fine teeth.

— *Benjamin Franklin*

Laundry

According to laundry room guidelines, a dryer of any kind must take exactly twice as long as the washing machine.

— *Jim Hoehn*

Lawyers

What's the difference between a good lawyer and a great lawyer? A good lawyer knows the law; a great lawyer knows the judge.

— *Anonymous*

Two farmers began to fight over the ownership of a cow. One began to pull from the head and the other from the tail. While they were doing this, a third came and began to milk the cow. He happened to be a lawyer.

— *Anonymous*

I get paid for seeing that my clients have every break the law allows. I have knowingly defended a number of guilty men. But the guilty never escape unscathed. My fees are sufficient punishment for anyone.

— *F. Lee Bailey*

You can tell an attorney by all the books of equal height on his shelf.

— *Dave Barry*

A lawyer's dream of heaven – every man reclaimed his property at the resurrection, and each tried to recover it from all his forefathers.

— *Samuel Butler*

If you cannot get your lawyer to call you, try not paying his bill.

— *Peter Ferguson*

When you have the facts on your side, argue the facts. When you have the law on your side, argue the law. When you have neither, holler.

— *Al Gore*

Lawyers believe a man is innocent until proven broke.

— *Robin Hall*

Daddy's a litigator. Those are the scariest kind of lawyers. Daddy's so good he gets $500 an hour to fight with people. But he fights with me for free because I'm his daughter.

— Cher Horowitz, Clueless

Laziness

Sometimes I get lazy and let the dishes stack up. But they don't stack too high. I've only got four dishes.

— Mark Fidych

Lectures

Most people tire of a lecture in ten minutes; clever people can do it in five. Sensible people never go to lectures at all.

— Stephen Leacock

Leftovers

A refrigerator is a place where you store leftovers until they are ready to be thrown out.

— Anonymous

Leftovers make you feel good twice. First, when you put them away, you feel thrifty and intelligent: "I'm saving food." Then a month later when blue hair is growing out of the ham, and you throw it away, you feel really intelligent: "I'm saving my life."

— George Carlin

My wife does wonderful things with leftovers. She throws them away.

— Herb Shriner

Leisure

Leisure time is when your wife can't find you.

— Anonymous

Leisure is the two minutes of rest a man gets while his wife is thinking up something else for him to do.

— Anonymous

There is no pleasure in having nothing to do; the fun is having lots to do and not doing it.

— *Andrew Jackson*

Lending

Don't lend money to friends – it causes amnesia.

— *Anonymous*

To improve your memory, lend people money.

— *Anonymous*

If you would lose a troublesome visitor, lend him money.

— *Benjamin Franklin*

Letters

One of the pleasures of reading old letters is the knowledge that they need no answer.

— *Lord Byron*

Life

There are two great rules of life: never tell everything at once.

— *Ken Venturi*

Lights

Have you any idea how many children it takes to turn off one light in the kitchen? Three. It takes one to say, "What light?" and two more to say, "I didn't turn it on."

— *Erma Bombeck*

Lines

Recent studies claim there are millions of adults who can't read or count – and if you don't believe it, take a look at the folks in front of you at the express checkout.

— *Anonymous*

I pick the loser every time. If you ever see me in a queue at the railway booking office, join the other one, because there'll be a chap at the front of mine who is trying to send a rhinoceros to Tokyo.

— *Basil Boothroyd*

At bank, post office or supermarket, there is one universal law which you ignore at your own peril: the shortest line moves the slowest.

— *Bill Vaughan*

Lipstick
Where lipstick is concerned, the important thing is not color but to accept God's final word on where your lips end.

— *Jerry Seinfeld*

Listening
Talk to a woman about herself and she will listen without interrupting.

— *Anonymous*

Women like silent men. They think they're listening.

— *Marcel Archard*

A good listener is generally thinking about something else.

— *Kin Hubbard*

If you want your children to listen, try talking softly – to someone else.

— *Ann Landers*

If you cannot get people to listen to you any other way, tell them it's confidential.

— *Patrick Murray*

Locks
I have six locks on my door, all in a row, and when I go out I only lock every other lock. Because I figure no matter how long somebody stands there and picks the locks, they're always locking three.

— *Elayne Boosler*

Losers
Loser: A lightning rod salesman who gets caught outside in a storm with a handful of samples.

— *Anonymous*

Losing

How to shake hands.

> — *Bettina Bunge, on what she learned from losing to Martina Navratilova eleven times in a row*

Welcome to the Lou Holtz Show. Unfortunately, I'm Lou Holtz.

> — *Lou Holtz, after his 1980 Arkansas team lost its fourth straight game*

Last season we couldn't win at home, and this season we can't win on the road. My failure as a coach is that I can't think of anyplace else to play.

> — *Harry Neale*

Love

A guy knows he's in love when he loses interest in his car for a couple days.

> — *Tim Allen*

When in love try not to say foolish things; if you succeed, you are not in love.

> — *Anonymous*

There is no reciprocity. Men love women, women love children, children love hamsters.

> — *Alice Ellis*

When you start having lunch and actually eating, it's already over.

> — *Erica Jong, on love*

Infatuation is when you think he's as sexy as Robert Redford, as smart as Henry Kissinger, as noble as Ralph Nader, as funny as Woody Allen and as athletic as Jimmy Connors. Love is when you realize that he's as sexy as Woody Allen, as smart as Jimmy Connors, as funny as Ralph Nader, as athletic as Henry Kissinger and nothing like Robert Redford – but you love him anyway.

> — *Judith Viorst*

Luck

I guess I was just in the right place at the right time.

> — *Cesar Geronimo, on being the 3,000th strikeout victim of Bob Gibson in 1974 and Nolan Ryan in 1980*

Do I believe in luck? Certainly! How else can you explain the success of those you detest?

— *Mark Twain*

Lust
He who looketh upon a woman loseth a fender.

— *Sign in auto repair shop*

He that but looketh on a plate of ham and eggs to lust after it, hath already committed breakfast with it in his heart.

— *C.S. Lewis*

Lying
Second story man: The fellow whose wife doesn't believe his first story.

— *Anonymous*

I don't know where Hank Aaron will break Ruth's record, but I can tell you one thing. Ten years from the day he hits it, three million people will say they were there.

— *Eddie Matthews*

When I was a little boy they called me a liar but now that I am a grownup they call me a writer.

— *Isaac Singer*

A lie is an abomination unto the Lord and a very present help in trouble.

— *Adlai Stevenson, quoting a child who had merged two memory verses*

Mail
Fragile is usually interpreted by postal workers as *please throw underarm.*

— *Harry Hershfield*

The Postal Service has gone from slow to inert. It's ironic that the only people in America unwilling to push the envelope are postal employees.

— *Dennis Miller*

Fifteen cents of every twenty-cent stamp goes for storage.

— *Louis Rukeyser*

Managers

A good manager knows that there is more than one way to skin a cat. A great manager can convince the cat that it's necessary.

— *Gene Perret*

Maps

Map: Handy schematic representation of all the various roads in the area which, unlike the one you are now on or are currently looking for, are large enough to be shown on a map.

— *Henry Beard and Roy McKie*

Take time when reading a map. When your partner is driving along an interstate, wait until the car has just passed the correct exit before stating firmly, "That was the right one."

— *Craig Brown*

Marriage

My toughest fight was with my first wife.

— *Muhammad Ali*

I married Miss Right. I just didn't know her first name was Always.

— *Anonymous*

A farmer put an ad in the papers that said, "Need wife who owns her own tractor. Please send picture of tractor."

— *Anonymous*

If you want your wife to pay undivided attention to every word you say, talk in your sleep.

— *Anonymous*

"All right, Victor, I know I'm not the perfect wife for you. I'm just outspoken."
  "By whom, dear?"

— *Anonymous*

A sure sign to tell if a guy is married to the girl is to notice the way he honks at her.

— *Anonymous*

Every mother generally hopes that her daughter will snag a better husband than she managed to do, but she's certain that her boy will never get as great a wife as his father did.

— *Anonymous*

When a man and woman marry they become one. The trouble starts when they try to decide which one.

— *Anonymous*

Some women spend the first part of their lives looking for a husband, and the last part wondering where he is.

— *Anonymous*

The diamond is the hardest stone . . . to get.

— *Anonymous*

You know the honeymoon is over when the husband takes his wife off the pedestal and puts her on a budget.

— *Anonymous*

Husbands choosing colors must have note from wives.

— *Sign in wallpaper and paint store*

I know what men want. Men want to be really, really close to someone who will leave them alone.

— *Elayne Boosler*

For years I was my own worst critic, then I got married.

— *Ron Dentinger*

I want a man who is kind and understanding. Is that too much to ask of a millionaire?

— *Zsa Zsa Gabor*

My wife and I made a bargain many years ago that in order to live harmoniously, I would decide all the major problems and she would decide all the unimportant problems. So far, in our 25 years of matrimony, we have never had any major problems.

— *Jonah Goldstein*

I love being married. I was single for a long time, and I just got so sick of finishing my own sentences.

— *Brian Kiley*

At every party there are two kinds of people – those who want to go home and those who don't. The trouble is, they are usually married to each other.

— *Ann Landers*

Yeah, but I love you more than football and basketball.
— *Tommy Lasorda, to his wife, who declared that he loved baseball and the Dodgers more than her*

The Japanese have a word for it. It's judo – the art of conquering by yielding. The Western equivalent of judo is "Yes, dear."

— *J.P. McEvoy*

When a man brings his wife a gift for no reason, there's a reason.

— *Molly McGee*

A man may be a fool and not know it – but not if he is married.

— *H.L. Mencken*

Marriage is the alliance of two people, one of whom never remembers birthdays and the other who never forgets.

— *Ogden Nash*

My wife and I have a deal. If I don't like the way she does something, I can do it myself.

— *Donny Osmond*

When a man opens the car door for his wife, it's either a new car or a new wife.

— *Prince Phillip*

A married couple can best be defined as a unit of people whose sleep habits are carefully engineered to keep each other awake.

— *Mary Roach*

Before marriage, a man will lie awake all night thinking about something you said; after marriage, he'll fall asleep before you finish saying it.

— *Helen Rowland*

When a man makes a woman his wife it's the highest compliment he can pay her and it's usually the last.

— *Helen Rowland*

When a girl marries, she exchanges the attentions of many men for the inattention of one.

— *Helen Rowland*

If your husband has difficulty in getting to sleep, the words, "We need to talk about our relationship" may help.

— *Rita Rudner*

Men who have a pierced ear are better prepared for marriage – they've experienced pain and bought jewelry.

— *Rita Rudner*

By all means marry; if you get a good wife, you'll be happy. If you get a bad one, you'll become a philosopher.

— *Socrates*

Love is blind – marriage is the eye-opener.

— *Pauline Thomason*

Mascara
Why can't women put on mascara with their mouth closed?

— *Peter Kay*

Maturity
The first sign of maturity is the discovery that the volume knob also turns to the left.

— *Anonymous*

Meat
Boy, the things I do for England.

— *Prince Charles, on sampling snake meat*

I did not say this meat was tough. I just said I didn't see the horse that usually stands outside.

— *W.C. Fields*

Meatloaf

I have a marvelous meatloaf recipe. All I do is mention it to my husband and he says, "Let's eat out."

— *Anonymous*

Meekness

The meek shall inherit the earth – if that's all right with you.

— *Anonymous*

Meetings

The two biggest problems in corporate America are making ends meet and making meetings end.

— *Anonymous*

The smart boss always has staff meetings at four in the afternoon on Friday. That way, nobody disagrees with him.

— *Anonymous*

The best way to kill an idea is to take it to a meeting.

— *Anonymous*

A meeting consists of people talking for hours to produce a result called minutes.

— *Milton Berle*

Whoever invented the meeting must have had Hollywood in mind. I think they should give Oscars for meetings: Best Meeting of the Year, Best Supporting Meeting, Best Meeting Based on Material from Another Meeting.

— *William Goldman*

Donuts: The only non-negotiable element to a successful meeting.

— *Joe Heuer*

The Law of Triviality means that the time spent on any item of the agenda will be in inverse proportion to the sum of money involved.

— *Cyril Parkinson*

Memoirs

Memoirs that's another Cherokee word; means when you put down the good things you ought to have done, and leave out the bad ones you did do.

— *Will Rogers*

Memory

Memory: What enables you to call a man by a name that's vaguely like his.

— *Anonymous*

My memory is starting to go. I locked the keys in my car the other day. Fortunately, I had forgotten to get out first.

— *Anonymous*

I went to my doctor about my loss of memory. He made me pay in advance.

— *Anonymous*

I'll never forget old what's-his-name.

— *Anonymous*

I write down everything I want to remember. That way, instead of spending a lot of time trying to remember what it is I wrote down, I spend the time looking for the paper I wrote it on.

— *Anonymous*

When you're on the sleeper at night, take your pocketbook and put it in a sock under your pillow. That way, the next morning you won't forget your pocketbook, 'cause you're looking for your sock.

— *Ping Bodie, advice to Yankee rookie George Halas in 1919*

First you forget names, then you forget faces. Next you forget to pull your zipper up and finally, you forget to pull it down.

— *George Burns*

Strangely, it was comforting to me when I read that squirrels forget where they hide about half their nuts.

— *Ruth Casey*

Memory is the thing you forget with.

— *Alexander Chase*

I have five boys, and they are all named George. If you want to be a good boxer, you've got to make preparations for the memory loss.

— *George Foreman*

Memory is a marvelous thing – it enables you to remember a mistake each time you repeat it.

— *Max Kauffmann*

The advantage of a bad memory is that one enjoys several times the same good things for the first time.

— *Friedrich Nietzsche*

Tonight we're going to consider one of the great questions of our time: Why the people who forget to turn off their car headlights always remember to lock the doors.

— *Robert Orben*

There are three things I always forget. Names, faces and – the third I can't remember.

— *Italo Svevo*

When I was younger I could remember anything, whether it happened or not.

— *Mark Twain*

Memos
A memorandum is written not to inform the reader but to protect the writer.

— *Dean Acheson*

In business, the memo is a way of transmitting information from those who have none to those who don't want any.

— Gene Perret

Men

What's the difference between an anniversary present and a golf ball? Guys will happily spend five minutes looking for a golf ball.

— Anonymous

Because I'm a man, I think what you're wearing is fine. I thought what you were wearing five minutes ago was fine too. Either pair of shoes is fine. With the belt or without it looks fine. Your hair is fine. You look fine. Can we just go now?

— Anonymous

You don't care if someone doesn't notice your new haircut.

— Anonymous, why it's great to be a man

You don't have to clean your apartment if the maid is coming.

— Anonymous, why it's great to be a man

You are unable to see wrinkles in your clothes.

— Anonymous, why it's great to be a man

One wallet and one pair of shoes, one color, all seasons.

— Anonymous, why it's great to be a man

You can leave the motel bed unmade.

— Anonymous, why it's great to be a man

You never have to drive to another gas station because this one's just too icky looking.

— Anonymous, why it's great to be a man

Christmas shopping can be accomplished for 25 relatives on December 24th in 45 minutes.

— Anonymous, why it's great to be a man

You can quietly watch a game with your buddy for hours without ever thinking, "He's mad at me."

— Anonymous, why it's great to be a man

Phone conversations are over in thirty seconds flat.

— Anonymous, why it's great to be a man

Question: How many men does it take to change a roll of toilet paper? Answer: Nobody knows, it's never been done.

— Anonymous

My ancestors wandered lost in the wilderness for forty years because even in biblical times, men would not stop to ask for directions.

— Elayne Boosler

Men build bridges and throw railroads across deserts, and yet they contend successfully that the job of sewing on a button is beyond them.

— Heywood Brown

When the waitress puts the dinner on the table, the old men look at the dinner. The young men look at the waitress.

— Gelett Burgess

The guy with the biggest stomach will be the first to take off his shirt at a baseball game.

— Glenn Dickey

What are the three words guaranteed to humiliate men everywhere? "Hold my purse."

— François Morency

Men do cry, but only when assembling furniture.

— Rita Rudner

Men and Women

A woman will say she's shopping when she hasn't bought a thing, and a man will say he's fishing when he hasn't caught a thing.

— Anonymous

A woman marries a man expecting he will change, but he doesn't. A man marries a woman expecting that she won't change, and she does.

— *Anonymous*

If a man yells in the woods and no woman hears him, is he still wrong?

— *Anonymous*

What women want: To be loved, to be listened to, to be desired, to be respected, to be needed, to be trusted and sometimes, just to be held.
    What Men Want: Tickets for the World Series.

— *Dave Barry*

Oh, I could make snide generalizations about women. I could ask why a woman would walk up to a perfectly innocent man who is minding his own business watching basketball and demand to know if a certain pair of pants makes her butt look too big, and then, no matter what he answers, get mad at him.

— *Dave Barry*

If you were standing in the middle of a bridge spanning a wilderness gorge, at the bottom of which was a spectacular white-water river, what would you do?
    Female Response: Admire the view.
    Male Response: Spit.

— *Dave Barry*

A man is a person who will pay two dollars for a one-dollar item he wants. A woman will pay one dollar for a two-dollar item she doesn't want.

— *William Binger*

When a woman goes to her closet and says, "I don't have anything to wear," she really means, "I don't have anything new to wear." When a man goes to his closet and says, "I don't have anything to wear," what he really means is, "I don't have anything clean to wear."

— *Diana Jordan and Paul Seaburn*

Women speak because they wish to speak, whereas a man speaks only when driven to speech by something outside himself – like, for instance, he can't find any clean socks.

— *Jean Kerr*

When a man says, "Honey, there are only two minutes left in the football game," it is the same amount of time as when his wife says, "Honey, I'll be ready in two minutes."

— *Ann Landers*

The trouble with women is that they never put the toilet seat back up.

— *Simon Nye*

When a man says "fine," he means everything's fine. When a woman says "fine," she means, "I'm really ticked off, and you have to find out why."

— *John Rogers*

When men and women agree, it is only in their conclusions; their reasons are always different.

— *George Santayana*

To sell something, tell a woman it's a bargain; tell a man it's deductible.

— *Earl Wilson*

Millionaires

A millionaire is the only person who receives letters from second cousins.

— *Anonymous*

What you do is begin as a billionaire. Then you go into the airline business.

— *Richard Branson, advice on becoming a millionaire*

My wife made me a millionaire. I used to have three million.

— *Bobby Hull*

I don't know much about being a millionaire, but I'll bet I'd be darling at it.

— *Dorothy Parker*

Misery

Misery no longer loves company. Nowadays it insists upon it.

— *Russell Baker*

Misery is when you make your bed and then your mother tells you it's the day she's changing the sheets.

— *Suzanne Heller*

Miss America

As Miss America, my goal is to bring peace to the entire world and then to get my own apartment.

— *Jay Leno*

Mistakes

Positive: Mistaken at the top of one's voice.

— *Ambrose Bierce*

Do you think you've learned from your mistakes?
    What mistakes?

— *Leslie Caron*

The fellow who says, "I may be wrong, but –," doesn't believe there can be any such possibility.

— *Kin Hubbard*

A man opened a new business and his best friend sent him a floral arrangement. The friend dropped in a few days later to visit his buddy and was pained to see that the flowers had a sign that read, "Rest in Peace." He called the florist to complain. The florist said, "It could be worse. Somewhere in this city is an arrangement in a cemetery that reads, 'Congratulations on your new location.'"

— *Charles Swindoll*

Modesty

Modesty is the hope that other people will discover by themselves how wonderful we really are.

— *Aldo Commarota*

A modest man is usually admired – if people ever hear of him.

— *Edgar Howe*

Money

The most popular labor-saving device today is still money.

— *Joey Adams*

If only God would give me some clear sign. Like making a large deposit in my name in a Swiss bank.

— *Woody Allen*

Will the person who lost a big fat roll of hundred dollar bills, wrapped in a rubber band, please report to the Lost and Found Department immediately. We found your rubber band.

— *Anonymous*

Self-fulfilling prophecy: Putting money away for an emergency.

— *Anonymous*

The easy way to teach children the value of money is to borrow from them.

— *Anonymous*

I'd just take up a collection.

— *Anonymous, policeman's response to the question, "How would you break up a crowd?"*

"I really don't want a lot of money," my neighbor's wife explained. "I just wish we could afford to live the way we're living now."

— *Anonymous*

A teenager lost a contact lens in his driveway while playing basketball. After a fruitless search, he told his mother the lens was nowhere to be found. Undaunted, she went outside and in a few minutes returned with the tiny lens in her hand. Her son asked "how did you manage to find it, Mom?" and the mom replied, "We weren't looking for the same thing; you were looking for a tiny piece of plastic; I was looking for $150."

— *Anonymous*

A smart father teaches his son how to make money, because he knows that somewhere a smart mother is teaching her daughter how to spend it.

— *Anonymous*

Most children's first words are "Mamma" or "Daddy." Mine were, "Do I have to use my own money?"

— *Erma Bombeck*

Money isn't everything, but it sure keeps you in touch with your children.

— *J. Paul Getty*

A billion dollars ain't what it used to be.

— *Nelson Bunker Hunt*

If you think nobody cares if you're alive, try missing a couple of car payments.

— *Ann Landers*

I started out with nothing and I've still got most of it left.

— *Groucho Marx*

There are a handful of people whom money won't spoil, and we all count ourselves among them.

— *Mignon McLaughlin*

A toy company is releasing Teacher Barbie this week. Apparently, it's like Malibu Barbie – only she can't afford the Corvette.

— *Stephanie Miller*

All I ask is the chance to prove that money can't make me happy.

— *Spike Milligan*

He knows money can't buy happiness, but that's alright with him. He likes money more than happiness anyway.

— *Gene Perret*

The shortest recorded period of time lies between the minute you put some money away for a rainy day and the unexpected arrival of rain.

— *Jane Quinn*

I'll tell you one good thing about money: it keeps the kids close to home.

— *Ken Venturi*

Please Lord, let me prove to you that winning the lottery won't spoil me.

— *Victoria Wood*

Monopolists

Monopolist: A man who keeps an elbow on each arm of the theater chair.

— *Anonymous*

Mother-in-laws

The young woman who gets on well with her mother-in-law probably can't afford a baby sitter.

— *Anonymous*

Mothers

Any mother could perform the jobs of several air traffic controllers with ease.

— *Lisa Alther*

A mother of seventeen children says that having another child is the only way she knows to keep the youngest child from being spoiled.

— *Anonymous*

The joy of motherhood: What a woman experiences when all the children are finally in bed.

— *Anonymous*

No matter how perfect your mother thinks you are, she will always want to fix your hair.

— *Suzanne Beilenson*

A mother is never cocky or proud, because she knows the school principal may call at any minute to report that her child has just driven a motorcycle through the gymnasium.

— *Mary Blakely*

I remember opening the refrigerator late one night and finding a roll of aluminum foil next to a pair of small red tennies. Certain that I was responsible for the refrigerated shoes, I quickly closed the door and ran upstairs to make sure I had put the babies in their cribs instead of the linen closet.

— *Mary Blakely*

I'm doing all the things my mother used to do that used to drive me crazy. I save twist ties from bread wrappers by the pound. I can't stand to be near a sweater without picking it up and folding it like they do in department stores. It's only a matter of time, I guess, before I put a fake flower on the antenna of my car at the shopping center.

— *Erma Bombeck*

Everybody else's mother. She has no name. Her phone number is unlisted. But she exists in the mind of every child who has ever tried to get his own way and used her as a last resort.

— *Erma Bombeck*

My sister said once: "Anything I don't want Mother to know, I don't even think of, if she's in the room."

— *Agatha Christie*

I love it when mothers get so mad they can't remember your name. "Come here, Roy, er, Rupert, er, Rutabaga . . . what is your name, boy? And don't lie to me, because you live here, and I'll find out who you are."

— *Bill Cosby*

A sweater is a garment worn by a child when the mother feels chilly.

— *Barbara Johnson*

Oh, to be only half as wonderful as my child thought I was when he was small, and only half as stupid as my teenager now thinks I am.

— *Rebecca Richards*

No matter how old a mother is, she watches her middle-aged children for signs of improvement.

— *Florida Scott-Maxwell*

One time I ran out of the store and took the bus home by myself after my mother asked a salesclerk where the *underpants* counter was. Everyone in the store heard her. I had no choice.

— *Phyllis Theroux*

A suburban mother's role is to deliver children: obstetrically once and by car forever after.

— *Peter de Vries*

A mother need only step into the shower to be instantly reassured she is indispensable to every member of her family.

— *Lynne Williams*

Mountains

Mountain climbers say they climb mountains "because they're there." Somebody ought to let them know that that's the same reason most of us go around them.

— *Anonymous*

Movies

In any war movie, never share a foxhole with a character who carries a photo of his sweetheart.

— *Del Close*

The length of a film should be directly related to the endurance of the human bladder.

— *Alfred Hitchcock*

I'm in the movie theater, a woman with an enormous head sits down directly in front of the person sitting next to me. I am amused, but only for a few seconds before she changes her mind and sits directly in front of me.

— *Rita Rudner*

All movie bartenders, when first seen, are wiping the inside of a glass with a rag.

— *David Smith*

Multitasking
Multitasking is the ability to screw everything up simultaneously.

— *Jeremy Clarkson*

Mushrooms
Mushrooms: Because they grow in damp places, they resemble umbrellas.

— *Anonymous, child's definition*

Music
Highbrow: A person who can listen to the *William Tell* overture without thinking of the *Lone Ranger*.

— *Anonymous*

I thought my son was playing his new compact disc, and then I discovered it was just a spoon caught in the garbage disposal.

— *Anonymous*

To do is to be.

— *Descartes*

To be is to do.

— *Voltaire*

Do be do be do.

— *Frank Sinatra*

I like both kinds of music – country and western.

— *John Belushi*

I can't wait to have a kid. I'll introduce them to classical music like Hendrix and the Rolling Stones.

— *Roger Howe*

Classical music is the kind that we keep thinking will turn into a tune.

— *Kin Hubbard*

Writing contemporary music isn't the problem – anyone can do that; it's enjoying it that's so difficult.

— *Miles Kington*

I am what you might call a prison singer – I never have the key, and I'm always behind a few bars.

— *Max Lucado*

Rap music sounds like someone feeding a rhyming dictionary to a popcorn popper.

— *Tom Robbins*

Too many pieces of music finish too long after the end.

— *Igor Stravinsky*

When I was a kid, I had no watch. I used to tell the time by my violin. I'd practice in the middle of the night and the neighbors would yell, "Fine time to practice the violin, three o'clock in the morning!"

— *Henny Youngman*

Musicians

What should you do when a musician comes to your door? Pay him and take your pizza.

— *Victor Borge*

I decided not to pursue a career as a professional musician because there's one sentence that has never been uttered: "Look! It's the banjo player's Porsche!"

— *Steve Martin*

Names

My name is Ebenezer –
'Tis a name I much despise;
And, oh, how quick I'll drop it
When rich Uncle Ebbie dies!

— *Anonymous*

Does the name Pavlov ring a bell?

— *Anonymous*

Little Jeffrey. I remember his name, not because he said, "I'm four years old," but because Jeffrey's mother said his name all 2,500 miles of the trip.

— *Bill Cosby*

Always end the name of your child with a vowel, so that when you yell, the name will carry.

— *Bill Cosby*

Any child can tell you that the sole purpose of a middle name is so he can tell when he's in trouble.

— *Dennis Fakes*

What can you do when you have a name that sounds like a disease?

— *Vitas Gerulaitis*

Darling: The popular form of address used in speaking to a person of the opposite sex whose name you cannot recall.

— *Oliver Herford*

My dad always told me one day I'd be glad I had that name because people would always remember it, but I'm not sure that day has come yet.

— *Nancy Hogshead*

My parents thought they were going to have a dog.

— *Sparky Lyle, on his nickname*

No, I'm breaking it in for a friend.

— *Groucho Marx, when asked if Groucho were his real name*

Until I was thirteen, I thought my name was "Shut Up."

— *Joe Namath*

My father is an undertaker, and I worked for him part-time. There were certain advantages to the job. For instance, while I was dating my wife I sent her flowers every day.

— *Digger Phelps, on how he got his nickname*

When I asked my dad about it, he told me that it had been a choice between that and Slide.

— *Golden Ruel, on his name*

Some days your child's middle name is "No!"

— *Dee Ann Stewart*

Great Funny Quotes

Naming our baby was a trial. I seize up when I have to name a document on my computer.

— *Jeff Stilson*

Nature
To me the outdoors is what you must pass through in order to get from your apartment into a taxicab.

— *Fran Lebowitz*

Negotiating
Swap: A trade between two people who think they skinned each other.

— *Anonymous*

The art of negotiation is something you learn at an early age. You'd be amazed how many teenagers get their first car by asking for a motorcycle.

— *James Hewett*

If you want a kitten, start out by asking for a horse.

— *Naomi, age fifteen*

Neighbors
Don't get annoyed if your neighbor plays his hi-fi at two o'clock in the morning. Call him at four and tell him how much you enjoyed it.

— *Anonymous*

Nervousness
He was as nervous as a long-tailed cat in a room full of rocking chairs.

— *Anonymous*

New York City
The only people here are the quick and the dead.

— *Billy Graham, on traffic in New York City*

Non-Conformists
Non-conformist: A person who keeps gloves in the glove compartment.

— *Anonymous*

Notes

Research notes: Things you keep for thirty years, then throw away the day before you need them.

— *Anonymous*

Offices

The company where I work provides four-foot-high cubicles so each employee can have some privacy. One day a co-worker had an exasperating phone conversation with one of her teenage sons. After hanging up, she heaved a sigh and said, "No one ever listens to me." Immediately several voices from surrounding cubicles called out, "Yes, we do."

— *Jo Jaimeson*

One executive had an office so large it could sleep ten, which made it perfect for staff meetings.

— *Gene Perret*

Opera

I do not mind what language an opera is sung in so long as it is a language I don't understand.

— *Sir Edward Appleton*

No opera plot can be sensible, for in sensible situations people do not sing.

— *Wystan Auden*

Aria is Italian for *a song that will not end in your lifetime.*

— *Dave Barry*

Opera is where a guy gets stabbed in the back, and instead of dying, he sings.

— *Robert Benchley*

People are wrong when they say that opera is not what it used to be. It is what it used to be. That is what is wrong with it.

— *Noel Coward*

Going to the opera, like getting drunk, is a sin that carries its own punishment with it.

— *Hannah More*

My experience with opera has been limited because of Nature's shortsightedness in the construction of the horse. Horses are simply not powerful enough to drag me into the presence of all that hog calling.

— *H. Allen Smith*

Sleep is an excellent way of listening to an opera.

— *James Stephens*

And now for my next trick. I'm going to make my boyfriend disappear. I say the magic word: opera.

— *Lea Thompson*

Opinions

To obtain a man's opinion of you, make him mad.

— *Oliver Wendell Holmes*

When I want your opinion I'll give it to you.

— *Laurence Peter*

You can always tell when a man's well-informed. His views are pretty much like yours.

— *Bob Phillips*

In all matters of opinion our adversaries are insane.

— *Mark Twain*

Optimists

Optimist: A bridegroom who thinks he has no bad habits.

— *Anonymous*

An optimist is a person who thinks he will never be a sucker again.

— *Anonymous*

An optimist is a man who hurries because he thinks his date is waiting for him.

— *Anonymous*

An optimist is a lady who puts her shoes on when the preacher says, "And now in conclusion."

— *Anonymous*

What's the definition of an optimist? An accordion player with a pager.

— *Anonymous*

An optimist is a man who will wink at a pretty girl and think that his wife won't see him.

— *Anonymous*

Optimist: A guy who can always see the bright side of other people's troubles.

— *Anonymous*

Optimist: A ninety-year-old man who is getting married and wants to buy a home near a school.

— *Anonymous*

Organized
She's not organized. She's insane. She's got a shoebox labeled, "Pieces of String Too Small to Use."

— *Frank Barone,* Everybody Loves Raymond

Others
We probably wouldn't worry about what people think of us if we could know how seldom they do.

— *Olin Miller*

Pace
Whenever I start to think the world is moving too fast, I go to the Post Office.

— *Billy Connolly*

Paddles
Paddle: Short, flat-bladed handheld oar used to keep the occupants of a canoe moist.

— *Henry Beard and Roy McKie*

Pain

Hi, coach. Isn't it wonderful that pain is only in the mind?

— Jerry Kramer, to Vince Lombardi, who was put in a neck brace after he fell

Paper

Paper is always strongest at the perforations.

— Carolyn Corry

Paranoids

You can learn a lot about paranoids just by following them around.

— Anonymous

Parenting

Frustrated wife to husband: "Next Sunday we'll trade jobs. You get the children fed and dressed, and I'll go out in the car and honk the horn for ten minutes."

— Anonymous

"I hear that God has sent you two more brothers."

"That's right. And I heard Dad say last night that He knows where the money's going to come from."

— Anonymous

Smear peanut butter on the sofa and curtains. Rub your hands in the wet flowerbed and then on the walls. Place a fish stick behind the couch and leave it there all summer. Congratulations, you are prepared for parenthood.

— Anonymous

Raising kids is part joy and part guerilla warfare.

— Ed Asner

In the end, the negative aspects of being a parent – the loss of intimacy, the expense, the total lack of free time, the incredible burden of responsibility, the constant nagging fear of having done the wrong thing, etc. – are more than outweighed by the positive aspects, such as never again lacking for primitive drawings to attach to your refrigerator with magnets.

— Dave Barry

Every person needs recognition. It is expressed cogently by the child who says, "Mother, let's play darts. I'll throw the darts and you say 'wonderful.'"
— *M. Dale Baugham*

Watching your daughter being collected by her date feels like handing over a million-dollar Stradivarius to a gorilla.
— *Jim Bishop*

One thing they never tell you about child raising is that for the rest of your life, at the drop of a hat, you are expected to know your child's name and how old he or she is.
— *Erma Bombeck*

I take a very practical view of raising children. I put a sign in each of their rooms: "Checkout Time Is 18 Years."
— *Erma Bombeck*

You know the only people who are always sure about the proper way to raise children? Those who've never had any.
— *Bill Cosby*

My parents never smiled . . . because I had brain damage. My wife and I don't smile because our children are LOADED with it. Oh, my parents smile now, whenever they come over to the house and see how much trouble I'm having. Oh, they have a ball! "Havin' a li'l trouble, huh, son?"
— *Bill Cosby*

Parents are not really interested in justice. They are interested in quiet.
— *Bill Cosby*

Every father says the same thing: "Where's your mother?"
— *Bill Cosby*

Parenthood: The state of being better chaperoned than you were before marriage.
— *Marcelene Cox*

When my father is asked to do a job or something around the house, he deliberately messes it up in the sure knowledge that my mother will stop him and say, "Oh, forget it, I'll do it myself."

— *Bob Hayden*

When your daughter's date shows up, casually show him your collection of five shrunken heads, then yell up to your daughter, "Honey, number six is here!"

— *David Letterman*

Insanity is hereditary – you get it from your children.

— *Sam Levenson*

The person in my household who seems to know the most about parenting is my ten-year-old daughter. Of course, she seems to know the most about everything under the sun. She will, undoubtedly, get smarter and smarter until the day she gives birth to her first child.

— *Karen Linamen*

Oh, what a tangled web do parents weave
    When they think that their children are naïve.

— *Ogden Nash*

Children aren't happy with nothing to ignore
    And that's what parents were created for.

— *Ogden Nash*

Parents

My parents were pleased that I was in the army. The fact that I hated it somehow pleased them even more.

— *Barry Humphries*

A man with parents alive is a fifteen-year-old boy.

— *Philip Roth*

Parking Spaces

Parking space: An unoccupied place on the other side of the street.

— *Anonymous*

The slowest drivers in the world are those people who are getting out of the parking space you want to get into.

— *Miles Kingston*

Parties

Nothing makes you more tolerant of a neighbor's noisy party than being there.

— *Franklin Adams*

When it comes to birthday parties it's easy to divide mothers into two groups: those who think that a birthday party for 24 five-year-old kids can be organized, educational and fun – and those who have had one.

— *Anonymous*

I have just returned from a children's party. I am one of the few survivors.

— *Percy French*

Hosting your child's party is like an exercise in riot control. Suddenly you find yourself spotting the ring leaders, appealing to the more moderate children to try and keep order, abandoning the living room to the mob and trying to consolidate your power base in the kitchen.

— *Jeremy Hardy*

How to throw a children's party: dig a pit, throw in the kids and ice cream, add chocolate sauce; an hour later take out and send home.

— *Tony Kornheiser*

Whoever named them *slumber parties* obviously never had one.

— *Karen Linamen*

Cocktail party: A device for paying off obligations to people you don't want to invite to dinner.

— *Charles Smith*

The main purpose of children's parties is to remind you that there are children worse than your own.

— *Katherine Whitehorn*

Great Funny Quotes

Patience

Patience is something you admire greatly in the driver behind you, but not in the one ahead of you.

— *Anonymous*

Lack of pep is often mistaken for patience.

— *Anonymous*

Patience: A minor form of despair, disguised as a virtue.

— *Ambrose Bierce*

It's easy finding reasons why other folks should be patient.

— *George Eliot*

Hoffstadler's Law: It always takes longer than you expect, even when you take Hoffstadler's Law into account.

— *Hoffstadler*

Patience and restraint are what parents have when there are witnesses.

— *Franklin Jones*

You can learn many things from children. How much patience you have, for instance.

— *Franklin Jones*

The world would be a better place if all men showed as much patience as they do when they're waiting for a fish to bite.

— *Bob Phillips*

Patience is the willingness to listen to the other person tell you his troubles before you tell him yours.

— *Herbert Prochnow*

Peace

The best way for a housewife to have a few peaceful moments to herself at the close of the day is to start doing the dishes.

— *Anonymous*

Honk if you love peace and quiet.

— Sign held up on a street corner

Universal peace sounds ridiculous to the head of an average family.

— Kin Hubbard

Peas
I've learned that if you spread the peas out on your plate, it looks like you ate more.

— Anonymous, age six

Pedestrians
Pedestrian: A guy who knows there are still several gallons of gas in the tank when the gauge shows empty.

— Anonymous

Pedestrian: A person who can't find the place where he parked his car.

— Anonymous

A pedestrian is a man who has two cars – one being driven by his wife, the other by one of his children.

— Robert Bradbury

People
The only normal people are the ones you don't know very well.

— Joe Ancis

God grant me the senility to forget the people I never liked, the good fortune to run into the ones I do and the eyesight to tell the difference.

— Anonymous

Those who resemble us we find good-looking, well set up, and above all charming.

— Jean de la Fontaine

Perfection

"Do you know someone perfect? Of course, not one of us does."

But then a hand went up.

"Do you mean to say you know of someone perfect?"

"Yes, my wife's first husband."

— Anonymous

The closest most people come to perfection is when they fill out a job application.

— Don Griffith

Perspective

The difference between us and other people is that their money looks bigger and their troubles smaller.

— Anonymous

Man is born with a tendency to detect a maximum of contributory negligence in other people's misfortunes, and nothing but blind chance in his own.

— Arthur Schnitzler

Pessimists

Always borrow from a pessimist – he never expects it back anyway.

— Anonymous

A pessimist is an optimist with experience.

— Chuck Daly

A lot of people become pessimists from financing optimists.

— C.T. Jones

Pets

All I've got at home is two dogs and four cats and six bunny rabbits and two parakeets and three canaries and a green parrot and a turtle and a bowl of goldfish and a cage of white mice and a silly old hamster. I want a squirrel!

— Roald Dahl

To keep a true perspective of your importance, you should have a dog that will worship you and a cat that will ignore you.

— *Rita Kubran*

Ferret, likes kids, nice pet, but chewed the guinea pig's ear off. Also, partially deaf guinea pig.

— *Bill Porter, newspaper ad*

My parents never wanted me to be upset about anything. They couldn't tell me when a pet had died. Once I woke up and my goldfish was gone. I asked, "Mom, where's Fluffy?" She said, "He ran away."

— *Rita Rudner*

Pianos

Play some Picasso.

— *Chris Morris, making a musical request to a piano player in a hotel bar*

When a piece gets difficult, make faces.

— *Artur Schnabel, advice to a fellow pianist*

Nothing soothes me more after a long and maddening course of piano recitals than to sit and have my teeth drilled.

— *George Bernard Shaw*

I wish the government would put a tax on pianos for the incompetent.

— *Edith Sitwell*

The early twilight of a Sunday evening in Hamilton, Bermuda, is an alluring time. There is just enough of whispering breeze, fragrance of flowers and sense of repose to raise one's thoughts heavenward; and just enough amateur piano music to keep him reminded of the other place.

— *Mark Twain*

Pillows

If women only have one head why do they need so many pillows? Am I missing something?

— *Anonymous*

Pizza

Four. I don't think I can eat eight.

> — *Yogi Berra, when asked whether he wanted his pizza cut into four*
> *or eight slices*

Planning

Dad showed me the importance of planning for the future by never throwing away anything that *might come in handy one day.*

> — *William Dane*

Planning: The art of putting off until tomorrow what you have no intention of doing today.

> — *Bob Phillips*

Play

Never play leapfrog with a unicorn.

> — *Anonymous*

The mother who can manage her children with dispatch can get them ready and sent to play with the youngsters next door before the youngsters there can get to her house.

> — *Anonymous*

PMS

My license plate says PMS. Nobody cuts me off.

> — *Wendy Liebman*

Poetry

Poetry: A literary gift – chiefly because you can't sell it.

> — *Anonymous*

Writing free verse is like playing tennis with the net down.

> — *Robert Frost*

Poet: A person born with an instinct for poverty.

> — *Elbert Hubbard*

For people who like that sort of thing, that is about the sort of thing they would like.

> — *Abraham Lincoln, responding to a young poet who had sent him some newly published poems with a request for his opinion of them*

My favorite poem is the one that starts "Thirty days hath September" because it actually tells you something.

> — *Groucho Marx*

Free verse: A device for making poetry easier to write and harder to read.

> — *H.L. Mencken*

It is easier to write a mediocre poem than to understand a good one.

> — *Michel de Montaigne*

Li Po wrote poems on rice paper and floated them down rivers until they sank out of sight. Contemporary poets publish their poems in little magazines. The results are much the same.

> — *Louis Phillips*

I've written some poetry I don't understand myself.

> — *Carl Sandburg*

I was working on the proof of one of my poems all morning, and took out a comma. In the afternoon I put it back again.

> — *Oscar Wilde*

Political Correctness

I'm sick and tired of everybody worrying about being politically correct. For instance, there are no more car thieves. Now they're nontraditional commuters. Homeless people are full-time outdoors men.

> — *Paul Rodriguez*

Politics

The little boy who goes to the store and forgets what his mother sent him for, will probably grow up to be a congressman.

> — *Anonymous*

You can always tell a good politician by the way he answers. He makes you forget the question.

— *Anonymous*

Prosperity: Something the businessmen create for the politicians to take credit for.

— *Anonymous*

When I was a kid, I knew that all fairy tales began with the line, "Once upon a time." Now that I'm grown up, I know that all fairy tales begin with the line, "If I'm elected . . ."

— *Anonymous*

In elections, when all is said and done, a lot more is said than done.

— *Anonymous*

I was so surprised in getting my nomination, I almost dropped my acceptance speech.

— *Anonymous*

Many a candidate feels that because his rival has been fooling the public for years, he should now be given a chance.

— *Anonymous*

When a man runs for Congress, you're a friend; when he's elected, you're a constituent; when he's legislating, you're a taxpayer.

— *Anonymous*

The cheapest way of tracing your family tree is to run for public office.

— *Anonymous*

There are three types of politicians: those that cannot lie, those that cannot tell the truth, and those that cannot tell the difference.

— *Anonymous*

There are two sides to every question – and a good politician takes both.

— *Anonymous*

You know you're out of power when your limousine is yellow and your driver speaks Farsi.

— *James Baker*

South Dakota is so underpopulated that merely by entering it you become a member of the state legislature.

— *Dave Barry*

Politics is the gentle art of getting votes from the poor and campaign funds from the rich, by promising to protect each from the other.

— *Peter Frame*

An old-time politician was once asked about an economic recession. "Son," he replied, "we don't have recessions in Texas. But I must admit, this is the worst boom we've had in years."

— *Criswell Freeman*

A politician is a person with whose politics you don't agree. If you agree with him, he is a statesman.

— *David George*

Successful politician: A person who can stand on a fence and make people believe it's a platform.

— *Joe Griffith*

The election isn't very far off when a candidate can recognize you from across the street.

— *Kin Hubbard*

They are the only friends I have who never pester me with their advice.
— *Andrew Jackson, on some ten-year-olds*

If one morning I walked on top of the water across the Potomac River, the headline that afternoon would read: PRESIDENT CAN'T SWIM.
— *Lyndon B. Johnson*

When politicians come up with a solution to your problem, you have two problems.

— *J. Kesner Kahn*

As I interpret President Eisenhower, we're now at the end of the beginning of the upturn of the downturn.

— *John F. Kennedy*

Mothers all want their sons to grow up to be president, but they didn't want them to become politicians in the process.

— *John F. Kennedy*

I asked each senator about his preferences for the presidency, and 96 senators each received one vote.

— *John F. Kennedy*

Forbes said he doesn't know yet whether he will run again for President or just fly his Lear jet over a forest fire and toss $60 million out the window.

— *Craig Kilborn*

Ninety percent of the politicians give the other ten percent a bad reputation.

— *Henry Kissinger*

Politician: One who is willing to do anything on earth for the workers except to become one.

— *Leonard Levinson*

Can you believe a candidate dropped out of the race because of a lack of campaign funds? Any politician who stops spending just because he's out of money doesn't belong in Washington anyway.

— *Kevin Nealon*

I must choose my words carefully in order to avoid any negative interpretation. Among politicians, this is a tactic known as lying.

— *Pat Paulsen*

Politicians are people who, when they see the light at the end of the tunnel, go out and buy more tunnel.

— *Sir John Quinton*

I think I'll demand a recount.

— *Ronald Reagan, on being advised just before he took office on the many problems that the country faced*

Recession is when your neighbor loses his job. Depression is when you lose yours. And recovery is when Jimmy Carter loses his.

— *Ronald Reagan*

Politics is not a bad profession. If you succeed there are many rewards; if you disgrace yourself, you can always write a book.

— *Ronald Reagan*

Before I refuse to take your questions, I have an opening statement.

— *Ronald Reagan*

You mean there aren't enough people mad at me already?
— *Ronald Reagan, on being presented with a referee's uniform during a visit from the NBA commissioner*

I can remember way back when a liberal was someone who was generous with his own money.

— *Will Rogers*

Coolidge was the only president nobody ever knew when he was acting, and when he wasn't. He was like a ukulele. You know, you can't ever tell when somebody is playing one, or just monkeying with it.

— *Will Rogers*

Politics ain't worrying this country one-tenth as much as finding a parking space.

— *Will Rogers*

In America any boy may become President and I suppose it's just one of the risks he takes.

— *Adlai Stevenson*

If you can't convince them, confuse them.

— *Harry S. Truman*

Whenever a fellow tells me he's bipartisan, I know he's going to vote against me.

— *Harry S. Truman*

Great Funny Quotes

That's a good question. Let me try to evade you.
— *Paul Tsongas, after being asked a question during his presidential run in '92*

Ponchos

Poncho: Portable sweat hut, steam room and sauna.
— *Henry Beard and Roy McKie*

Popularity

What makes certain people popular? That depends. In third grade, it's the simple ability to stuff two dimes up your nose.
— *Dennis Miller*

Positive Thinking

A positive attitude may not solve all your problems, but it will annoy enough people to make it worth the effort.
— *Herm Albright*

I was going to buy a copy of *The Power of Positive Thinking*, and then I thought: "What good would that do?"
— *Ronnie Shakes*

Poverty

Poverty is hereditary – you get it from your children.
— *Phyllis Diller*

There's another advantage of being poor – a doctor will cure you faster.
— *Kin Hubbard*

Practice

If you think practice makes perfect, you don't have a child taking piano lessons.
— *Anonymous*

A driving range is a place where golfers go to get all the good shots out of their system.
— *Henry Beard*

I never really believed in spring practice. It doesn't tell you anything. It was like having your daughter come in at four o'clock in the morning with a Gideon Bible.

— *Duffy Daugherty*

My mother used to pitch to me and my father would shag balls. If I hit one up the middle, close to my mother, I'd have some extra chores to do. My mother was instrumental in making me a good hitter.

— *Eddie Matthews*

Praise

Praise: Something a person tells you about yourself that you've suspected all along.

— *Anonymous*

We bestow on others praise in which we do not believe, on condition that in return they bestow upon us praise in which we do.

— *Jean Rostand*

Prayer

So far today, God, I've done all right. I haven't gossiped; lost my temper; been greedy, grumpy, nasty, selfish or even overindulgent. I'm really glad about that. But, in a few minutes, God, I'm going to get out of bed and from then on I'm probably going to need a lot more help. Thank you.

— *Anonymous*

Pray for me!

— *Anonymous, shouted to the congregation by a misbehaving young child being carried to the exit by his father during a church service*

When I was a youngster, I used to have to kneel and pray for long periods with my grandfather, who prayed aloud in an unintelligible mutter. One day I finally found the courage to tell him that I couldn't understand a word of his prayers. My grandfather slowly lifted up his head and looked at me with disdain. "I wasn't talking to you," he retorted.

— *Bill Cosby*

Prayer never seems to work for me on the golf course. I think this has something to do with my being a terrible putter.

— *Billy Graham*

Some golfers pray, and unquestionably derive great benefit from it. Continual prayer on the golf course, continual repetition of the same prayer will enable any golfer, at the end of six months, to know that prayer by heart.

— *Buddy Hackett*

It's a little frustrating sometimes when you listen to your children saying their prayers. It costs thousands and thousands of dollars to raise them and you get mentioned ahead of the goldfish but after the gerbil.

— *Pat Williams and Ken Hussar*

Preachers

Two clergymen talking:
"When I preach, I have the congregation glued to their seats."
"Now, why didn't I think of that!"

— *Anonymous*

Preacher: A person who talks in someone else's sleep.

— *Anonymous*

The English church-goer prefers a severe preacher because he thinks a few home truths will do his neighbors no harm.

— *George Bernard Shaw*

Predicament

Predicament: The wage of consistency.

— *Ambrose Bierce*

Pregnancy

Mother's Preparation for Pregnancy: From the food co-op, obtain a 25-pound bag of pinto beans and attach it to your waist with a belt. Wear it everywhere you go for nine months. Then remove ten of the beans to indicate the baby has been born.

— *Anonymous*

Never tell a woman that you didn't realize she was pregnant unless you're certain that she is.

— *Dave Barry*

When I had reached my term, I looked like a rat dragging a stolen egg.

— *Colette*

By far the most common craving of pregnant women is not to be pregnant.

— *Phyllis Diller*

I feel like a man building a boat in his basement which he may not be able to get out through the door.

— *Abigail Lewis, on being pregnant*

The biggest problem facing a pregnant woman is not nausea or fatigue or her wardrobe – it's free advice.

— *Sophia Loren*

A pregnant woman wants toasted snow.

— *Hebrew proverb*

All the time during the pregnancy when I was supposed to be reading baby books and taking classes didn't go totally to waste because I did use the time to shop for the perfect video camera.

— *Paul Riser*

I envy the kangaroo. That pouch setup is extraordinary; the baby crawls out of the womb when it is about two inches long, gets into the pouch and proceeds to mature. I'd have a baby if it would develop in my handbag.

— *Rita Rudner*

Preteens
A preteen is sort of like having a tornado before a hurricane hits.

— *W. Bruce Cameron*

Price
I paid too much for it, but it's worth it.

— *Samuel Goldwyn*

People want economy, and they will pay any price to get it.

— *Lee Iacocca*

Pride

Even though I knew better, when my son's first tooth came through early, I was proud of him, and I was proud of me. It was perfectly clear to me how absurd this was. I said to myself, "This is ridiculous. It's his tooth. He didn't make it. I didn't make it. It just came." Then I called up two friends and bragged about the precocious tooth.

— *Polly Berends*

I never cease to amaze myself. I say this humbly.

— *Don King*

If the general had known how big a funeral he would have had, he would have died years ago.
— *Abraham Lincoln, on a recently deceased public figure known for his vanity*

The night we won the World Series, I was understandably feeling my oats. I asked my wife how many really great managers she thought there were in baseball. Glaring at me, she said, "I think there's one less than you do."
— *Danny Murtaugh*

Blessed is the man who does not insist upon talking about his children when I want to talk about mine.

— *Roy Smith*

Problems

If you're not confused then you don't understand what's going on.
— *Anonymous*

When trouble arises and things look bad, there is always one individual who perceives a solution and is willing to take command. Very often, that person is crazy.

— *Dave Barry*

It often happens that I wake up at night and begin to think of a serious problem and decide that I must tell the pope about it. Then I wake up completely and remember that I am the pope.

— *Pope John XXIII*

Why can't life's problems hit us when we're seventeen and know everything?
— *A.C. Jolly*

What a pity human beings can't exchange problems. Everyone knows exactly how to solve the other fellow's.

— *Olin Miller*

The chief cause of problems is solutions.

— *Eric Sevareid*

Procrastination
Tomorrow: A husband's greatest labor-saving device.

— *Anonymous*

Children never put off till tomorrow what will keep them from going to bed tonight.

— *Anonymous*

There is nothing quite so valuable as work. That's why it's a good idea to leave some for tomorrow.

— *Marian Dolliver*

Prodigies
A child prodigy is one with highly imaginative parents.

— *Anonymous*

Progress
Whenever man comes up with a better mousetrap, nature immediately comes up with a better mouse.

— *James Carswell*

Projects
If a project requires n components, there will be n-1 units in stock.
— *Robert Mueller*

Psychologists
Psychologist: A man who, when a voluptuous girl enters a room, watches the other men's reactions.

— *Anonymous*

Not every child psychologist is a bachelor, but every bachelor is a child psychologist.

— *Anonymous*

Publishing
The way British publishing works is that you go from not being published no matter how good you are, to being published no matter how bad you are.

— *Tibor Fischer*

Puddles
Puddle: A Small body of water that draws other small bodies wearing dry shoes into it.

— *Anonymous*

Punctuality
It's easy to tell those who have never had much experience in committee work – they always get to the meeting on time.

— *Anonymous*

Punctuality: The art of guessing how late the other person is going to be.

— *Anonymous*

One good thing about punctuality is that it's a sure way to help you enjoy a few minutes of privacy.

— *Orlando Battista*

I am a believer in punctuality, though it makes me lonely.

— *E.V. Lucas*

I have often noticed that the people who are late are often so much jollier than the people who have to wait for them.

— *E.V. Lucas*

I've been on a calendar, but never on time.

— *Marilyn Monroe*

The trouble with being punctual is that there's nobody there to appreciate it.

— *Harold Rome*

My Aunt Minnie would always be punctual and never hold up production, but who would pay to see my Aunt Minnie?
> — *Billy Wilder, on Marilyn Monroe's unpunctuality*

Puns
A pun is the lowest form of humor, unless you thought of it yourself.
> — *Doug Larson*

Quartets
A quartet is where all four think the other three can't sing.
> — *Anonymous*

Questions
A child can ask a thousand questions that the wisest man cannot answer.
> — *Jacob Abbott*

When a child asks difficult questions, invention is the necessity of Mother.
> — *Anonymous*

The essential skill of parenting is making up answers. When an experienced father is driving down the road and his kid asks him how much a certain building weighs, he doesn't hesitate for a second. "Three thousand, four hundred and fifty-seven tons," he says.
> — *Dave Barry*

The most popular question for small children is "Why?" They can use it anywhere and it's usually impossible to answer:
    Child: "What's that?"
    You: "It's a goat."
    Child: "Why?"
> — *Dave Barry*

While I was on a shopping spree in a department store, I heard a five-year-old talking to his mother on the down escalator. He asked, "Mommy, what do they do when the basement gets full of steps?"
> — *Hal Linden*

Great Funny Quotes

You know children are growing up when they start asking questions that have answers.

— *John Plomp*

Someone – probably now in a padded cell somewhere – once documented the fact that preschoolers ask 437 questions a day. It should be noted that 437 per day was simply the average number of questions. Many children – probably yours included – ask this many before breakfast.

— *Sandi Shelton*

Like the sands on the beach are the sentences that begin with "why?"

— *Dee Ann Stewart*

Quiet
Quiet does not necessarily mean you don't need to worry.

— *Anonymous, things I've learned from my children*

Quotations
If you want to be quoted, say something you shouldn't say.

— *Anonymous*

Now we sit through Shakespeare in order to recognize the quotations.

— *Orson Welles*

Racehorses
A racehorse is the only creature that can take thousands of people for a ride at the same time.

— *Anonymous*

One way to stop a runaway horse is to bet on him.

— *Jeffrey Bernard*

To own a racehorse is the equivalent of burning a yacht on the front lawn every year.

— *Adam Nicholson*

Rain
Timing has a lot to do with the outcome of a rain dance.

— *Anonymous*

Two longtime golfers are standing overlooking a river. One golfer turns to the other and says, "Look at those idiots fishing in the rain."

— *Anonymous*

Question: What normally follows two days of rain?
Answer: Monday.

— *Ron Dentinger*

Raingear

Raingear: Lightweight, waterproof clothing that would have provided a player excellent protection from a sudden downpour out on the course if it weren't in the trunk of his car.

— *Henry Beard and Roy McKie*

Reading

I took a speed-reading course where you run your finger down the middle of the page and was able to read *War and Peace* in twenty minutes. It's about Russia.

— *Woody Allen*

No one who can read is ever successful at cleaning out an attic.

— *Anonymous*

Realists

You may be sure that when a man begins to call himself a realist, he is preparing to do something that he is secretly ashamed of doing.

— *Sydney Harris*

Reasons

A man always has two reasons for what he does – a good one, and the real one.

— *J.P. Morgan*

Rebellion

There comes a time when rebellious young people should take their turn as adults against whom the next wave of youngsters can rebel.

— *D. Sutten*

Great Funny Quotes

Receptionists

The receptionist is the first person you see when you visit an office, and the last person you see when you leave. And if she does her job right, she's sometimes the only person you see while you're there.

— *Gene Perret*

You must have received a message like this sometime: "A Mr. Somebody called – I didn't catch his name – and he didn't give me a chance to jot down the number. The message had something to do with life or death or something like that. Call him."

— *Gene Perret*

Recipes

A recipe is a series of step-by-step instructions for preparing ingredients you forgot to buy in utensils you don't own to make a dish the dog won't eat the rest of.

— *Henry Beard*

Referees

The trouble with referees is that they just don't care which side wins.

— *Tom Canterbury*

Our coach loves the refs. He sends them cards every Christmas – in Braille.

— *Anonymous*

References

A bad reference is as hard to find as a good employee.

— *Robert Half*

Relationships

There's no easy way to break off any relationship. It's like the mozzarella cheese on a good slice of pizza. No matter how far you pull the slice away from your mouth it just gets thinner and longer but never snaps.

— *Jerry Seinfeld*

To symbolize our great relationship, I'd like you to have this framed x-ray of my ulcer.

— *Pat Williams, submitting his resignation to 76ers owner Harold Katz*

Relatives

A man I know solved the problem of too many visiting relatives. He borrowed money from the rich ones and loaned it to the poor ones. Now none of them come back.

— Bob Phillips

The rich never have to seek out their relatives.

— Italian proverb

Relativity

When a man sits with a pretty girl for an hour, it seems like a minute. But let him sit on a hot stove for a minute, and it's longer than any hour. That's relativity.

— Albert Einstein

Remorse

Remorse: A miscalculation of the chances of detection.

— Anonymous

Repairmen

If you wait for a repairman, you will wait all day. If you go out for five minutes, he will arrive and leave while you are gone.

— Arther Bloch

Repairs

Fixing something *for now* means that it is as fixed as it's going to get with tape. There will be no more fixin' until it falls apart again. At that time it can be fixed *for now* again.

— Kevin Nealon, on what his father taught him

Repartee

Backward, turn backward, O Time in thy flight,
    Just thought of a comeback I needed last night.

— Les Dawson

Repartee is something we think of 24 hours too late.

— Mark Twain

Report Cards

Son, there's one thing in your favor. With these grades, you couldn't possibly be cheating.

— *Anonymous*

Father: "Let me see your report card."

Son: "You can't. My friend just borrowed it. He wants to scare his parents."

— *Anonymous*

Here's my report card . . . and I'm tired of watching TV anyway.

— *Bob Phillips*

Requests

When a person tells you, "I'll think it over and let you know" – you know.

— *Olin Miller*

Research

Research means they are looking for the guy who lost the file.

— *Leonard Levinson*

Responsibility

I know God will not give me anything I can't handle. I just wish He didn't trust me so much.

— *Mother Teresa*

Restaurants

Nobody goes there anymore. It's too crowded.

— *Yogi Berra*

The longer the description on the menu, the less you will get on your plate.

— *Shirley Lowe*

In restaurants, the hardness of the butter increases in direct proportion to the softness of the bread.

— *Harriet Markman*

The quality of food in a restaurant is in inverse proportion to the number of signed celebrity photographs on the wall.

— *Bryan Miller*

That chap over there is having soup and it sounds delicious.

— *Eric Morecambe and Ernie Wise*

Can we just get rid of wine lists? Do we really need to be reminded every time we go out to a nice restaurant that we have no idea what we're doing? Why don't they just give us a trigonometry quiz with the menu?

— *Jerry Seinfeld*

No matter how many good tables at a restaurant are free, you will always be given the worst available.

— *Jonathan Yardley*

Résumé

A résumé is a balance sheet without any liabilities.

— *Robert Half*

Retirement

When a rookie asked me if he could take my daughter out on a date.

— *Reggie Lemelin, on when he knew it was time to retire*

I know some people who were tempted to take an early retirement, but they couldn't. They needed the rubber bands.

— *Gene Perret*

One manager made the following presentation to a retiring employee: "We wanted to give you something you've had your eye on since you began working here." Then he gave him the clock on the wall.

— *Gene Perret*

Retreating

Gentlemen. We are not retreating. We are merely advancing in another direction.

— *General O.P. Smith*

Reunions

Class reunion: A gathering where you come to the conclusion that most of the people your own age are a lot older than you are.

— Anonymous

Your high school reunion. You get that letter in the mail. You feel like you only have six months to make something of yourself.

— Drew Carey

A class reunion is a meeting where 200 people hold in their stomachs for five hours while writing down the names and addresses of friends they'll never contact.

— Brenda Davidson

Revenge

If your enemy offends you, give his child a drum.

— Fran Lebowitz

Rich

An advantage of being rich is that all your faults are called eccentricities.

— Anonymous

A rich man's joke is always funny.

— Heywood Broun

The good thing about being rich is when you drop a Tic Tac, you don't have to pick it up – until nobody's looking.

— Jack Cooke

When you're rich, people say you're profound, handsome, graceful – and sing like an angel.

— Jewish proverb

Make money and the whole world will conspire to call you a gentleman.

— Mark Twain

Roller Skating

I have recently taken up two new sports: roller-skating and ankle-spraining, in that order.

— *Miles Kington*

Romance

All the world loves a lover, except those who are waiting to use the phone.

— *Anonymous*

Love will find you, even if you are trying to hide from it. I have been trying to hide from it since I was five, but the girls keep finding me.

— *Bobby, age eight, when asked what it's like to fall in love*

Lovers will just be staring at each other and their food will get cold. Other people care more about the food.

— *Brad, age eight, when asked how you can tell if two adults eating dinner at a restaurant are in love*

Tell them that you own a whole bunch of candy stores.

— *Del, age six, when asked what was a surefire way to make a person fall in love with you*

I made no advances to her, but she accepted them.

— *Louis Scutenaire*

Rules

There are no exceptions to the rule that everybody likes to be an exception to the rule.

— *William F. Buckley, Jr.*

The rule book is only good for you when you go deer hunting and run out of toilet paper.

— *Billy Martin*

Rumors

Washington is the place where nobody believes a rumor until it has been officially denied.

— *Anonymous*

Great Funny Quotes

Running

When I first started running, I was so embarrassed, I'd walk when cars passed me. I'd pretend I was looking at the flowers.

— *Joan Samuelson*

Salary

The paycheck is the company's way of saying "Thank you." Most of us, of course, wish they would say it louder.

— *Gene Perret*

Most people work up the courage to ask for a raise by remembering that it takes less nerve to ask for the increase than it does to go home and tell your spouse that you couldn't work up the nerve.

— *Gene Perret*

Salesmen

First salesman: "I made some valuable contacts today."
    Second salesman: "I didn't get any orders either."

— *Anonymous*

I used to sell furniture for a living. The trouble was, it was my own.

— *Les Dawson*

The person who agrees with everything you say either isn't listening to you or plans to sell you something.

— *Bud Holiday*

Sandwiches

I told them sandwiches.

— *George Foreman, on what he likes to build*

Santa Claus

If your child asks how Santa Claus gets into the house, just tell him he comes in through a large hole in Daddy's wallet.

— *Anonymous*

The three stages of a man's life:
1) He believes in Santa Claus;
2) He doesn't believe in Santa Claus;
3) He is Santa Claus.

— *Anonymous*

Our kids have reached the age where they're beginning to get suspicious about Santa Claus. This morning one of them asked me how he could get all those millions and millions of different things into one bag. I said, "You ever look in your mother's purse?"

— *Robert Orben*

Schedules
Schedule: That wonderful little gimmick which enables a housewife to do approximately one half of the things she had planned.

— *Anonymous*

School
"The teacher said I must learn to write more legibly," the kid told his mother, "but if I do, she'll find out I can't spell."

— *Joey Adams*

First of all I learned that my name isn't "Pumpkin" – it's "Karla."
— *Anonymous, kindergarten student, when asked what she learned the first day of school*

So, what did you do in school today?
I broke in my purple clogs.

— *Mel and Cher Horowitz,* Clueless

As long as there are algebra exams, there will be prayer in schools.

— *Anonymous*

The happiest days of your life are the school days, provided your children are old enough to attend.

— *Anonymous*

If you promise not to believe everything your child says happens at school, I'll promise not to believe everything he says happens at home.

— *Anonymous, teacher*

Everyone is in awe of the lion tamer in a cage with a half-dozen lions – everyone but a school bus driver.

— *Anonymous*

I know how we can solve our national crisis in educational funding: Whenever the schools need money, they could send a letter to all the parents, saying, "Give us a contribution right now, or we're going to hold a Science Fair." They'd raise billions.

— *Dave Barry*

Newton's First Law of Inertia states, "A body at rest will remain at rest until 8:45 p.m. the night before the science-fair project is due, at which point the body will come rushing to the body's parents, who are already in their pajamas, and shout, 'I just remembered the science fair is tomorrow and we gotta go to the store right now!'"

— *Dave Barry*

When I was a kid I never went to school – I said I was sick – but I always managed to get better by 3:30 – I'd run into the kitchen – "Look, Ma – a miracle happened! I'm well! A little angel came and sat on my bed – she touched me with a wand and said, 'Go out and play.'"

— *Bill Cosby*

Nothing grieves a child more than to study the wrong lesson and learn something he wasn't supposed to.

— *E.C. McKenzie*

Professor: "This essay on your dog is, word for word, the same as your brother's."
　　Student: "Yes, sir, it's the same dog."

— *Mildred Meiers and Jack Knapp*

As children grow attached to their teachers and classmates, they can finally say goodbye to their mothers without reenacting the death scene from *Camille.*

— Sue Mittenthal

I'd like to say a few words about one of the most popular concepts in modern education – show and tell. Show and tell is a device created by grammar schools to communicate family secrets to 32 other families before 9:15 in the morning.

— Robert Orben

Sam had just completed his first day at school. "What did you learn today?" asked his mother. "Not enough," said Sammy. "I have to go back tomorrow."

— Joseph Rosenbloom

For every person who wants to teach there are approximately thirty who don't want to learn.

— W.C. Sellar and R.J. Yeatman

I will not conduct my own fire drills.
I will not conduct my own fire drills.
I will not conduct . . .

— Bart Simpson, The Simpsons

The hot lunch is always spaghetti on school picture day.

— Dee Ann Stewart

Screens
Screens: The wire mesh that keeps flies from getting out of the house.

— Anonymous

Secretaries
Secretary: A person who can tell by a caller's name whether or not the boss is in.

— Anonymous

I can please only one person a day. Today is not your day. Tomorrow isn't looking good either.

— Sign on a secretary's desk

Secretary wants job; no bad habits; willing to learn.

— *Want ad*

Secrets

Most of us can keep a secret. It's the people we tell it to who can't.

— *Anonymous*

Secret: Something you tell to one person at a time.

— *Anonymous*

Wild horses couldn't drag a secret out of most women; however, women seldom have lunch with wild horses.

— *Ivern Boyett*

A woman can keep one secret – the secret of her age.

— *Voltaire*

Self-esteem

Low Self-esteem Support Group will meet Thursday at 7:00 p.m. Please use the back door.

— *Church bulletin*

I have an inferiority complex. But it's not a very good one.

— *Steven Wright*

Sermons

A good sermon helps people in a couple of ways. Some rise from it greatly strengthened. Others wake from it refreshed.

— *Anonymous*

A preacher must know that his sermon,
   That points to the heavenly portal,
   Need not be totally eternal,
   Just to be eternally immortal.

— *Anonymous*

The average man's idea of a good sermon is one that goes over his head and hits a neighbor.

— *Anonymous*

It was a divine sermon. For it was like the peace of God – which passeth all understanding. And like His mercy, it seemed to endure forever.

— Henry Hawkins

I don't like to hear cut-and-dried sermons. When I hear a man preach I like to see him act as if he were fighting bees.

— Abraham Lincoln

Sewage

Why do they bother saying *raw sewage?* Do some people actually cook that stuff?

— George Carlin

Shins

Shin: A device used for finding furniture in the dark.

— Anonymous

Shoes

A shoe store is where a woman tries on many pairs of shoes, hoping to find something larger in the same size.

— Anonymous

High heals – invented by a woman who had been kissed on the forehead.

— Anonymous

Then there was the wife who could not understand why her husband would go into a store and buy the first pair of shoes he tried on, just because he happened to like them.

— Anonymous

If the shoe fits, it's the wrong color.

— Anonymous

The ideal shoe for the career woman is the basic pump with a *sensible* heel, by which I mean a heel that will just fit through the holes in a standard street grate.

— Dave Barry

The amount of time it takes for you to leave the house in the morning is directly proportional to the number of shoes in your closet.

— Leigh Anne Jasheway

Put kitty litter in your shoes, and it'll take away the odor. Unless, of course, you own a cat.

— Jay Leno

What do women want? Shoes.

— Mimi Pond

The black nose of a shoe would peek from beneath the hem of the Sisters of Mercy's full habit, then dart back inside the flaring recesses, as though each was sheltering a family of mice.

— Richard Selzer

If you want to forget all your troubles, wear shoes that are too tight.

— Mildred Watts

Shopping

Shopping Preparation: Herd a flock of goats through the grocery store. Always keep every goat in sight and bring enough money to pay for whatever they eat or destroy.

— Anonymous

I knew this was going to be a good day when I walked into the supermarket and found a shopping cart with all the wheels going in the same direction.

— Anonymous

You do not want the one you can afford.

— Scott Baker, Baker's Law of Economics

Anything you buy will go on sale next week.

— Erma Bombeck

A woman does not spend all her time buying things; she spends part of it taking them back.

— Edgar Howe

Why does my wife want me to go shopping with her? She knows I'm no good at it. She's going to want to do stuff like try different things on. Soon as she comes out of the dressing room with the first thing on, to me it's like a bank robbery. "Let's go!"

— *Ritch Shydner*

Short

That's why I'm so doggone short. He keeps patting me on the top of the head whenever I do something right.

— *Mary Lou Retton, on her coach, Bela Karolyi*

Show Business

Show business is dog-eat-dog. It's worse than that. It's dog-doesn't-return-the-other-dog's-phone-calls.

— *Woody Allen*

In 1956 the population of Los Angeles was 2,243,901. It had risen to 2,811,801 by 1970. 1,650,917 of them are currently up for a series.

— *Fran Lebowitz*

I handed in a script last year and the studio didn't change one word. The word they didn't change was on page 87.

— *Steve Martin*

Signatures

A signature always reveals a man's character – and sometimes even his name.

— *Evan Essar*

Sin

A preacher announced that there were 86 kinds of sin. The following week he was besieged with requests for the list.

— *Anonymous*

Sins of commission are the sins we commit, and the sins of omission are those we meant to commit but forgot.

— *Anonymous, child*

Singers

You know you're going out with someone too young for you when they say, "Did you know Paul McCartney was in a band before Wings?"

— *Anonymous*

You know what would end Madonna's career? If enough parents suddenly started to like her.

— *Bill Cosby*

Somebody gave me a Bob Dylan tape for Christmas. One good thing about Bob Dylan: When the batteries run down in my Walkman he still sounds the same.

— *Lance Crouther*

I went to watch Pavarotti once. He doesn't like it when you join in.

— *Mitch Miller*

You got to have smelt a lot of mule manure before you can sing like a hillbilly.

— *Hank Williams*

Sisters

Big sisters are the crabgrass in the lawn of life.

— *Charles Schulz*

The typewriter when played with expression, is not more annoying than the piano when played by a sister.

— *Oscar Wilde*

Skill

Skill: Describing a great drive or long, difficult putt by one's self. Contrast with act of God, which describes a great drive or long, difficult putt by an opponent.

— *Paul Dickson*

He that is good with a hammer tends to think everything is a nail.

— *Abraham Maslow*

Skinny

Manute is so skinny, they save money on road trips – they just fax him from city to city.

— *Woody Allen, on 7'7" Manute Bol*

Sleep

Nothing makes a bed more comfortable than the ringing of an alarm clock.

— *Anonymous*

The hardest thing in the world to raise is a child – especially in the mornings.

— *Anonymous*

People who say they sleep like a baby usually don't have one.

— *Leo Burke*

If you want the world to beat a path to your door, just try to take a nap on a Saturday afternoon.

— *George Burns*

To a new father, a nap is a basic need, and he soon learns that this need can best be met in a local theater.

— *Bill Cosby*

The amount of sleep required by the average person is about five minutes more.

— *Max Kauffmann*

There is nobody who is thirstier than a four-year-old who has just gone to bed.

— *Fran Lebowitz*

When two people go to bed together at the same time, the one that snores will fall asleep first.

— *Laurence Peter*

He snored so loud that we thought he was driving his hogs to market.

— *Jonathan Swift*

I can remember the first time I had to go to sleep. Mom said, "Steven, time to go to sleep." I said, "But I don't know how." She said, "It's real easy. Just go down to the end of tired, and hang a left." So I went down to the end of tired, and just out of curiosity I hung a right. My mother was there, and she said, "I thought I told you to go to sleep."

— *Steven Wright*

Snobs

I'm not a snob. Ask anybody. Well, anybody who matters.

— *Simon Le Bon*

Soccer

I knew we were in trouble when we got there and their cheerleaders were bigger than us.

— *Matt McDonagh, after his elementary school soccer team was elimi-nated in the city playoffs*

Sociologists

The parable of the Good Samaritan for sociologists: A man was attacked and left bleeding in a ditch. Two sociologists passed by, and one said to the other, "We must find the man who did this – he needs help."

— *Anonymous*

Soldiers

You can always tell an old soldier by the inside of his holster and cartridge boxes. The young ones carry pistols and cartridges: the old ones, grub.

— *George Bernard Shaw*

Solitude

Solitude: The state of being closer to nature than to the nearest flush toilet.

— *Henry Beard and Roy McKie*

Songs

It's annoying to have a song running through your mind all day that you can't stop humming. Especially if it's something difficult like *Flight of the Bumblebee.*

— *George Carlin*

To write songs, I usually need a reason. Like not having any money.

— *Willie Nelson*

The remaining Beatles will release yet another new song using previously recorded vocals by John Lennon. The song will be called "We're Not Home Right Now; Leave a Message After the Beep."

— *Colin Quinn*

Anything too stupid to say is sung.

— *Voltaire*

Sons

You know your son is growing up when he starts looking at girls the same way he used to look at dessert.

— *Anonymous*

I am waging a battle with my son to keep him normal, defined as "like me, but with less nose hair."

— *Dave Barry*

I must admit I did ask God to give me a son because I wanted someone to carry the family name. Well, God did just that and I now confess that there have been times when I've told my son not to reveal who he is.

— *Bill Cosby*

I am on my way to Massachusetts, where I have a son at school, who, if report be true, already knows much more than his father.

— *Abraham Lincoln*

Sophistication

Sophistication: Liking something you don't like.

— *Anonymous*

Spaghetti

Spaghetti can be eaten most successfully if you inhale it like a vacuum cleaner.

— *Sophia Loren*

Spare Tires

Spare tire: The one you don't check until you have a flat.

— Anonymous

Speeches

Orator: An unpopular wind instrument.

— Anonymous

The toastmaster is the person who rises after the dinner and tells you the best part of the evening is over.

— Anonymous

After eating, the sense of hearing is temporarily dulled, which is nature's way of protecting man from after-dinner speakers.

— Anonymous

Most speakers don't need an introduction, just a conclusion.

— Anonymous

Listen up, because I've got nothing to say and I'm only going to say it once.

— Yogi Berra

I do not object to people looking at their watches when I am speaking. But I strongly object when they start shaking them to make certain they are still going.

— Lord Birkett

He was a practiced orator and could make a very small amount of information go a long way.

— George Birmingham

I'm honored to be the first sitting President to address a community college commencement. Recognizing this is a grand occasion, I wanted some tips from the best speaker I know – so I went to the First Lady, Laura. I asked her what I should talk about, and she said, "You ought to talk about fifteen minutes."

— George W. Bush

I wish I could remember my halftime speech so I could forget it.
> — *David Davitch, Idaho football coach, on losing to Weber State 42-21 after leading 21-14 at halftime*

I have a new theory of eternity.
> — *Albert Einstein, while listening to a long-winded after-dinner speaker*

Blessed is the man who, having nothing to say, abstains from giving us wordy evidence of the fact.
> — *George Eliot*

I guess I should warn you, if I turn out to be particularly clear, you've probably misunderstood what I've said.
> — *Alan Greenspan*

My job is to talk to you, and your job is to listen. If you finish first, please let me know.
> — *Harry Herschfield*

Why doesn't the fellow who says, "I'm no speechmaker," let it go at that instead of giving a demonstration.
> — *Kin Hubbard*

Hubert, a speech, to be immortal, doesn't have to be eternal.
> — *Muriel Humphrey, to her husband*

The human brain starts working the moment you are born and never stops until you stand up to speak in public.
> — *Sir George Jessel*

This is a moment that I deeply wish my parents could have lived to share. My father would have enjoyed what you have so generously said of me – and my mother would have believed it.
> — *Lyndon B. Johnson*

Before I speak, I have something important to say.
> — *Groucho Marx*

What orators lack in depth they make up in length.

— *Baron de La Montesquieu*

A speaker who does not strike oil in ten minutes should stop boring.

— *Louis Nizer*

"In conclusion" – the phrase that wakes up the audience.

— *Herbert Prochnow*

Gentlemen, you have just been listening to that Chinese sage, On Too Long.

— *Will Rogers*

I'm here to speak, and you're here to listen, and if you finish before me, feel free to leave.

— *Adlai Stevenson*

I've given hundreds of talks over the years. One thing I've learned is that the most popular speaker is often the person who follows "Thank you for that nice introduction" by saying soon afterward, "So in conclusion . . ."

— *John Wooden*

Spelling

Misspellers of the world – UNTIE!

— *Anonymous*

Whatever you do, don't learn to spell *cat* – because if you do, after that the words just get harder and harder.

— *Anonymous, age seven, giving his younger brother advice on starting school*

The little girl assured her teacher, "Of course I know how to spell banana. I just never know when to stop."

— *Bennett Cerf*

I'm allergic to spelling.

— *Barney Salzberg*

Spinach

I said, "Eat your spinach. Think of the thousands of kids who would love some."

My son said, "Name two!"

— Anonymous

How to eat spinach like a child. Divide into piles. Rearrange again into piles. After five or six maneuvers, sit back and say you are full.

— Delia Ephron

Sports

Go Braves! And take the Falcons with you.

— Bumper sticker in Atlanta

Do your homework, because you'll never make money riding a bike.

— Greg LeMond's high-school teacher

If there is a group of men doing anything with a ball in a field, another group of men will watch.

— Jasmine Birtles

Money is the driving force in college sports. If NBC tells Notre Dame to kick off at 3:00, all they ask is, "a.m. or p.m.?"

— Beano Cook

The smaller the ball used in the sport, the better the book. There are superb books about golf, very good books about baseball, not very many good books about basketball, and no good books on beach balls.

— George Plimpton

My husband is so confident that when he watches sports on television, he thinks that if he concentrates he can help his team. If the team is in trouble, he coaches the players from our living room, and if they're really in trouble, I have to get off the phone in case they call him.

— Rita Rudner

Sportswriters
Here's a twenty, bury two.
> — *Bear Bryant, on being asked to chip in ten dollars to help cover the cost of a sportswriter's funeral*

Here's a dime. Call all your friends.
> — *Tom Meany, to an unpopular sportswriter*

Sprouts
Kids will eat anything – snot, scabs, soil, earwax, toenail clippings. But not sprouts.
> — *Tony Burgess*

Statistics
The use to which statistics are sometimes put reminds us that ever since they put those Smokey the Bear ads in the New York subways there hasn't been a single forest fire in Manhattan.
> — *Anonymous*

Statistics always remind me of the fellow who drowned in the river whose average depth was only three feet.
> — *Woody Hayes*

Statistics show that of those who contract the habit of eating, few survive.
> — *Wallace Irwin*

Smoking is one of the leading causes of statistics.
> — *Fletcher Knebel*

He uses statistics as a drunken man uses lampposts – for support rather than for illumination.
> — *Andrew Lang*

Status Quo
Status Quo: Latin for the mess we're in.
> — *Ronald Reagan*

Stockbrokers

A stockbroker is someone who takes all your money and invests it until it's gone.

— *Woody Allen*

Wall Street is the only place that people ride to in a Rolls Royce to get advice from those who take the subway.

— *Warren Buffett*

I did so bad this year, I had to switch brokers – from stock to pawn.

— *Gene Perret*

Stories

The trouble with telling a good story is that it invariably reminds the other fellow of a dull one.

— *Sid Caesar*

When a fellow says, "Well, to make a long story short," it's already too late.

— *Don Herold*

Stubbornness

Firmness: That admirable quality in ourselves that is detestable stubbornness in others.

— *Anonymous*

Stubbornness we deprecate,
    Firmness we condone.
    The former is my neighbor's trait,
    The latter is my own.

— *Anonymous*

Success

Success: Something that always comes faster to the man your wife almost married.

— *Anonymous*

A person whose ship has come in usually finds most of his relatives at the dock.

— *Anonymous*

Success is relative. The more success, the more relatives.

— *Anonymous*

There's no secret about success. Did you ever know a successful man that didn't tell you all about it?

— *Kin Hubbard*

Behind every successful man stands a surprised mother-in-law.

— *Hubert Humphrey*

Suffering

It is easier to suffer in silence if everyone knows about it.

— *Anonymous*

Summer

Summer: The time of year that children slam the door they left open all winter.

— *Anonymous*

It's a sure sign of summer if the chair gets up when you do.

— *Walter Winchell*

Swimming Pools

Family swimming pool: A small body of water completely surrounded by other people's children.

— *Anonymous*

Sympathy

Sympathy: What you give a friend or relative when you don't want to lend him money.

— *Anonymous*

When you are in trouble, people calling to sympathize are really only looking for the particulars.

— *Edgar Howe*

Synonyms

Is there another word for *synonym*?

— *Anonymous*

A synonym is a word you use when you can't spell the other one.

— *Baltasar Gracián*

Talking
What's the use of teaching your kid to talk when in a few years you'll wish he'd shut up.

— *Anonymous*

Breath is what a mother holds when her youngster starts telling a neighbor about some family incident.

— *Anonymous*

When your mind quits working, don't forget to turn off the sound.

— *Anonymous*

A child learns to talk in about two years, but it takes about sixty years for him to learn to keep his mouth shut.

— *Anonymous*

As soon as your children learn to talk, there will be no such thing as a family secret.

— *Jim Hoehn*

There's nothing wrong with having nothing to say – unless you insist on saying it.

— *Bob Phillips*

Thomas Edison did not invent the first talking machine. He invented the first one you could turn off.

— *Herbert Prochnow*

Parents of teens and parents of babies have something in common. They spend a great deal of time trying to get their kids to talk.

— *Paul Swets*

Tall
He looks like a pair of pliers.

— *Johnny Bench, on the lanky Von Hayes*

I can't miss a class. The professor doesn't have to call the roll to know I'm not there.

> — *Tom Burleson, 7'4", on his days at North Carolina State*

No – I clean giraffe ears.

> — *Elvin Hayes, 6'11", asked if he was a basketball player*

If you go to movies with him, you get in for half price.

> — *Johnny Kerr, on the 7'2" Mark Eaton*

They always tell you how tall the kid is going to be when he grows up. The one mother wrote that her son was 6 feet but she knew he would be taller because he had an uncle 6'8". I told her we would just recruit the uncle.

> — *Abe Lemons*

I want all you kids to focus on just one thing: grow taller.

> — *Debbie Leonard, Duke University basketball coach, advising her team*

I'm not on a ladder.

> — *Willis Reed, to Jim Wergeles, Knicks' publicist, who found out that the 6'11" Reed was painting his ceiling and cautioned him not to fall off the ladder*

I told my team not to worry about Shaquille O'Neal. He puts his pants on the same way we do, only four feet higher.

> — *Billy Tubbs*

No basketball coach cares about the height of the players as long as their ears pop when they stand up.

> — *Dick Vitale*

Taxes

Did you ever notice? When you put the two words *The* and *IRS* together it spells *THEIRS*.

> — *Anonymous*

If Patrick Henry thought that taxation without representation was bad, he should see how bad it is *with* representation.

— *Anonymous*

The attitude of Congress toward hidden taxes is not to do away with them but just to hide them better.

— *Anonymous*

The three Rs of the Internal Revenue Service: This is ours; that is ours; everything is ours.

— *Anonymous*

Why does a small tax increase cost you two hundred dollars and a substantial tax cut save you thirty cents?

— *Peg Bracken*

Tax reform is taking the taxes off things that have been taxed in the past and putting taxes on things that haven't been taxed before.

— *Art Buchwald*

President Herbert Hoover returned his salary to the government. His idea caught on and now we're all doing it.

— *Sam Ewing*

Why sir, there is every possibility that you will soon be able to tax it.
— *Michael Faraday, when asked about the usefulness of electricity*

April fifteenth is the day when you get to pay for the government you've been complaining about all year long.

— *Gene Perret*

Someday they may come out with a real simplified tax form: "Send us everything you've got. You can owe us the rest."

— *Gene Perret*

The IRS sent back my tax return saying I owed eight hundred dollars. I said, "If you'll notice, I sent a paper clip with my return. Given what you've been paying for things lately, that should more than make up the difference."

— *Emo Philips*

The taxpayer – that's someone who works for the federal government but doesn't have to take a civil service exam.

— *Ronald Reagan*

The difference between death and taxes is that death doesn't get worse every time Congress meets.

— *Roy Schaefer*

Teachers

Experience is a great teacher, and sometimes a pretty teacher is a great experience.

— *Evan Esar*

Parents never really appreciate teachers until it rains all weekend.

— *Bob Goddard*

Teaching

It's noble to teach oneself. It is nobler to teach others, and less trouble.

— *Mark Twain*

Teamwork

Teamwork: A chance to blame someone else.

— *Ambrose Bierce*

Teenagers

Any astronomer can predict with absolute accuracy exactly where every star in the universe will be at 11:30 tonight. He can make no such prediction about his teenage daughter.

— *James Adams*

I saw a teenager who had a ring in her nose, her eyebrow and a stud through her tongue. She looked like she had fallen face first into a tackle box.

— *Anonymous*

The only way to recapture your youth is to take the car keys away from him.

— *Anonymous*

Don't tell a teenager that her hair looks like a mop; she probably doesn't know what a mop is.

— Anonymous

Teenage: When youngsters aren't bright enough to realize their parents couldn't be that stupid.

— Anonymous

Puberty is the period when students stop asking questions and begin questioning answers.

— Anonymous

Raising teenagers is like nailing Jell-O to the wall.

— Anonymous

Remember how the news media made a big deal about it when those people came out after spending two years inside Biosphere 2? Well, two years is nothing. Veteran parents assure me that teenagers routinely spend that long in the bathroom.

— Dave Barry

Family life got better and we got our car back – as soon as we put "I love Mom" on the license plate.

— Erma Bombeck

I'm trying very hard to understand this generation. They have adjusted the timetable for childbearing so that menopause and teaching a sixteen-year-old how to drive a car will occur in the same week.

— Erma Bombeck

Signs you may be living with a teenager: your car insurance suddenly costs more than your car, your gas tank is always empty and your laundry basket is always full.

— W. Bruce Cameron

"Where are you going?"
   "Out."
   "Out's kind of a big place. Wanna narrow that down?"
   "Side."

— *Teddie Cochran and Max Ryan*

This is my diagram of the teenage brain: me, me, me – you, if you can do something for me.

— *Jane Condon*

Telling a teenager the facts of life is like giving a fish a bath.

— *Arnold Glasgow*

There's nothing wrong with teenagers that reasoning with them won't aggravate.

— *Jean Kerr*

It isn't what a teenager knows that worries his parents. It's how he found out.

— *Ann Landers*

No need to worry about your teenagers when they're not at home. A national survey revealed that they all go to the place – *out* – and they all do the same thing – *nothing*.

— *Bruce Lansky*

Few things are more satisfying than seeing your children have teenagers of their own.

— *Doug Larson*

I know a teenage girl who had been trying to run away from home for a year but every time she gets to the front door the phone rings.

— *Bob Phillips*

See what will happen to you if you don't stop biting your fingernails.
   — *Will Rogers, message written on a postcard of the Venus de Milo that he sent to his young niece*

Get out of my life, but first could you take me and Cheryl to the mall?

— *Anthony Wolf*

Telekinetic Powers

How many people here have telekinetic powers? Raise my hand.

— *Emo Philips*

Telephones

My teenage daughter picked up the phone and only talked for thirty minutes. "Why so short?" I asked. "It was a wrong number," she replied.

— *Anonymous*

Physics lesson: When a body is submerged in water, the phone rings.

— *Anonymous*

I owe my great learning to the fact that I have always kept an open book on my desk which I read whenever somebody on the phone says, "One moment please."

— *Helen Daley*

When our phone rings it's always for our daughter. When it isn't ringing it's because she's talking on it. Sometimes when she's on our phone the neighbors will come over and tell her she's wanted on their phone.

— *Art Frank*

Utility is when you have one telephone, luxury is when you have two, opulence is when you have three — and paradise is when you have none.

— *Doug Larson*

Remember that as a teenager you are at the last stage in your life when you will be happy to hear that the phone is for you.

— *Fran Lebowitz*

The only thing I ever said to my parents when I was a teenager was "Hang up, I got it!"

— *Carol Leifer*

Great Funny Quotes

"I'll call you right back." This is more of a verbal tic than a lie. If you're one of those people who are still waiting for the return call, you shouldn't.

— *Mark McCormack*

How does that phone cord get so tangled? All I do is talk and hang up. I don't pick it up and do a cartwheel and a somersault.

— *Larry Miller*

Wives are people who think it's against the law not to answer the phone when it rings.

— *Rita Rudner*

Television

I watch about six hours of TV a day. Seven if there's something good on.

— *Bart Simpson,* The Simpsons

A child is someone who stands halfway between an adult and a TV set.

— *Anonymous*

Why do you press harder on a remote control when you know the battery is dead?

— *Anonymous*

Over ninety percent of high school students think BC means Before Cable.

— *Argus Hamilton*

With high definition TV, everything looks bigger and wider. Kind of like going to your 25th high school reunion.

— *Jay Leno*

Men don't care what's on TV. They only care what else is on TV.

— *Jerry Seinfeld*

Men seem to flip around the television more than women. Women will stop and go, "Well let me see what the show is before I change the channel. Maybe we can nurture it, work with it, help it grow into something." Men don't do that. Because women nest and men hunt.

— *Jerry Seinfeld*

I found a snake in my yard and got a shovel and whacked the heck out of it. Then I didn't have cable for a week.

— *Charlie Viracola*

Temptations

Opportunity may knock only once, but temptation leans on the doorbell.

— *Anonymous*

Most people want to be delivered from temptation but would like it to keep in touch.

— *Robert Orben*

Resisting temptation is easier when you think you'll probably get another chance later on.

— *Bob Talbert*

There are several good protections against temptations, but the surest is cowardice.

— *Mark Twain*

Tennis

I was at a boys' tournament in Ocala where nine matches were going on at a time, and it sounded like a pigsty.

— *Bobby Curtis, on the grunting at a juniors tennis tournament*

I wasn't so upset the other day when a letter came addressed to "Dave the Dope." That's the privilege of all sports fans, but how did the post office know where to deliver it?

— *Dave Freed*

When the best player at your club calls you out of the blue and invites you to play tennis, he probably wants to sell you life insurance.

— *Barry Tarshis*

Theater

Long experience has taught me that in England nobody goes to the theater unless he or she has bronchitis.

— *James Agate*

In the theater the audience wants to be surprised – but by things that they expect.

— *Tristan Bernard*

Hamlet is a terrific play, but there are way too many quotations in it.

— *Hugh Leonard*

A drama critic is a person who surprises a playwright by informing him what he meant.

— *Wilson Mizner*

Theft

The government wrote a startling report on petty office theft, then found out they had no loose-leaf binders left to put it in.

— *Gene Perret*

Thoughts

As a child you never quite understood how your mom was able to know exactly what you were thinking. Sometimes Mom would know what you were thinking before the thought entered your head. "Don't even think about punching your brother," she would warn before you had time to make a fist.

— *Linda Sunshine*

Tigers

An explorer says a tiger will not hurt you if you carry a white walking cane. We suppose you must carry it real fast.

— *Anonymous*

Time

An appointment at 9:00 a.m.? You mean to say, there are two nine o'clocks?

— *Tallulah Bankhead*

There is never enough time, unless you're serving it.

— *Malcolm Forbes*

Toasters

Our toaster has two settings – too soon or too late.

— *Sam Levenson*

Today

Why is tomorrow always getting here before I'm through with today?

— Dennis the Menace, as he's being carted off to bed against his will

Tools

Any tool dropped while repairing a car will roll beneath the vehicle to its exact center.

— Anonymous

The man who has a full set of tools has no children.

— Anonymous

You need only two tools in life: WD-40 and duct tape. If it doesn't move and it should, use WD-40. If it moves and it shouldn't, use the tape.

— Anonymous

When working on a project, if you put away a tool that you're certain you're finished with, you will need it instantly.

— Arther Bloch

Tornados

A tornado touched down, uprooting a large tree in the front yard and demolishing the house across the street. Dad went to the door, opened it, surveyed the damage, and muttered, "Darned kids . . ."

— Tim Conway

Tourists

Tourists are alike: They all want to go places where there are no tourists.

— Anonymous

A tourist is someone who goes 3,000 miles to get a photograph of themselves in front of their car.

— Robert Benchley

Toys

If you wonder where your child left his roller skates, try walking around the house in the dark.

— Leopold Fechtner

Everyone who ever walked barefoot into his child's room late at night hates Legos.

— *Tony Kornheiser*

An unbreakable toy is good for breaking other toys.

— *John Peers*

Nothing brings out a toddler's devotion to a toy she has abandoned more quickly than another child playing with it.

— *Robert Scotellaro*

Growing up was rough. Most of the responsibility for my ever-growing family was up to me. Joyce would not leave my side. Carl had eye problems. Betsy lost a leg. Finally I said, "I cannot raise any more stuffed animals; I have no time to myself." Eventually they all left home to join the Salvation Army.

— *Wendy Spero*

The minute a toy goes in the garage sale is the minute it becomes their favorite.

— *Dee Ann Stewart*

A three-year-old child is a being who gets almost as much fun out of a $56 set of swings as it gets out of finding a small green worm.

— *Bill Vaughan*

I'd say half of our Lego has been through this kid.

— *Reese Wilkerson*

Track and Field

At the summer Olympic Games, a girl bumped into a guy carrying an eight-foot stick.

"Excuse me," said the girl, "but are you by any chance a pole vaulter?"

"Nein, I'm a German, but how did you know my name is Valter?"

— *Anonymous*

We do not have cross-country and we do not have pole vaulting.

— *Gerard Curtin, on the annual field day at Sing-Sing Prison*

Traffic Lights

What is happening when you hear varoom ... screech, varoom ... screech, varoom ... screech?

A moron is trying to drive through an intersection with a flashing red light.

— *Anonymous*

Despite the fact that computer speeds are measured in nanoseconds and picoseconds – one billionth and one trillionth of a second, respectively – the smallest interval of time known to man is that which occurs between the traffic light turning green and the driver behind you blowing his horn.

— *Johnny Carson*

The quickest way to make a red light turn green is to try to find something in the glove compartment.

— *Gary Doney*

As the light changed from red to green to amber and back to red again, I sat there thinking about life. Was it nothing more than a lot of honking and yelling? Sometimes it seemed that way.

— *Jack Handey*

The first one to see the light turn green is the driver of the second car back.

— *Terry Marchal*

The red light is always longer than the green light.

— *Laurence Peter, Peter's Theory of Relativity*

Trains

The next train left ten minutes ago.

— *Anonymous*

The only way of catching a train, I discovered, is to miss the train before.

— *G.K. Chesterton*

Travel

A child will fall asleep in the car five minutes before you reach your destination.

— *Anonymous*

The journey of a thousand miles begins with a broken fan belt and a leaky tire.

— *Anonymous*

A nickel will get you on the subway, but garlic will get you a seat.

— *New York Jewish saying*

Seasickness comes in two stages – in the first, you're afraid you're going to die; in the second, you're afraid you're not going to.

— *Sandi Toksvig*

Truth

If you want to hear the whole truth about yourself, anger your neighbor.

— *Anonymous*

The truth hurts – maybe not as much as jumping on a bike with the seat missing.

— *Lt. Frank Drebin,* Naked Gun 2 1/2

A person with no children says, "Well I just love children," and you say "Why?" and they say, "Because a child is so truthful, that's what I love about 'em – they tell the truth." That's a lie, I've got five of 'em. The only time they tell the truth is if they're having pain.

— *Bill Cosby*

Umbrellas

Umbrella: A collapsible device carried all over the golf course on sunny days, and left at home when it rains.

— *Anonymous*

A businessman needs three umbrellas – one to leave at the office, one to leave at home and one to leave on the train.

— *Paul Dickson*

Umpires

I never questioned the integrity of an umpire – their eyesight . . . yes.

— *Leo Durocher*

I occasionally get birthday cards from fans. But it's often the same message: They hope it's my last.

— *Al Forman, National League umpire*

Well, then I think you are doing a lousy job.

— *Cleon Jones, after he asked an umpire if he could get thrown out for thinking and the umpire said no*

When I said "You're a disgrace to mankind," I was talking to myself, not the umpire.

— *John McEnroe*

I couldn't see well enough to play when I was a boy, so they gave me a special job – they made me the umpire.

— *Harry S. Truman*

Uncertainty

The certainty of misery is better than the misery of uncertainty.

— *Walt Kelly*

Vacations

If you didn't go on a vacation this year, you can get the feel of one by tipping every third person you see.

— *Anonymous*

He planned to go on a vacation and forget everything. The first time he opened his suitcase, he discovered how nearly he had succeeded.

— *Anonymous*

We went to Niagara Falls recently with several other families, and our feeling of awe and wonderment can best be summed up by the words of my friend Libby Burger, who, when we first beheld the heart-stopping spectacle of millions of gallons of water per second hurtling over the gorge below, said, "I have to tinkle."

— *Dave Barry*

Don't you love looking at your friends' vacation pictures? Especially when they owe you money.

— *J. Chris Newberg*

Vacuum Cleaning

Men and dogs are alike in that both have irrational fears about vacuum cleaning.

— Anonymous

When Sears comes out with a riding vacuum cleaner, then I'll clean the house.

— Roseanne Barr

I have a friend who once proposed that, as a quick *touch-up* measure, you could cut a piece of two-by-four the same width as the vacuum cleaner and drag it across the carpet to produce those little parallel tracks, which as far as Clint could tell were the major result of vacuuming.

— Dave Barry

Nature abhors a vacuum. And so do I.

— Anne Gibbons

Carperpetuation: The act, when vacuuming, of running over a string at least a dozen times, reaching over and picking it up, examining it, then putting it back down to give the vacuum one last chance.

— Rich Hall

Verbal

Verbal: Able to whine in words.

— Anonymous

Vice Presidents

Once there were two brothers. One ran away to sea, the other was elected vice president, and nothing was ever heard from either of them again.

— Thomas Marshall, U.S. vice president

The whole convention has degenerated into nothing but a dogfight for vice president. Men who two days ago wouldn't even speak to a vice president, are now trying to be one.

— Will Rogers

I am against vice in every form, including the vice presidency.

— *Morris Udall, on being asked if he would accept the vice presidential nomination*

The vice presidency is sort of like the last cookie on the plate. Everybody insists he won't take it, but somebody always does.

— *Bill Vaughan*

Wagons

That was very important, the wagon. Just as important as wheels are today. Because if the wagon broke down and you were too dumb or lazy to fix it, that's where you stayed. You don't think people headed out for Tulsa, do you? You know, everywhere you see a nice big spread in America, they got two broken wheels outside.

— *Gallagher*

Waiters

Some waiters discuss the menu with you as if they were sharing wisdom picked up in the Himalayas.

— *Seymour Britchky*

I'd complain about the service if I could find a waiter to complain to.

— *Mel Calman*

When I was growing up, my father told me I'd make a great waiter. They never come when you call them.

— *Bob Monkhouse*

Gimme a table near a waiter.

— *Henny Youngman*

Washington State

I won't say it's remote up here, but my last speech was reviewed in *Field & Stream*.

— *George Raveling, on coaching at Washington State*

Wastebaskets

Wastebasket: Something to throw things near.

— *Anonymous*

Waterbeds

A king-size waterbed holds enough water to fill a 2,000 square foot house four inches deep.

— *Anonymous, things I've learned from my children*

Water-skiers

A small girl watching a water-skier said to her father, "That man is silly. He'll never catch that boat."

— *Anonymous*

Weather

Four days of perfect weather begin on Monday.

— *Henry Beard*

Weather: There is no way to be sure the sun will come out, but showing up at the golf club in hip boots, a plastic raincoat and an umbrella will certainly point things in the right direction.

— *Martin Ragaway*

Weddings

Planning a wedding is not all that difficult, provided you do almost nothing else for the better part of a year. But as you go through it, you must make sure, amid all the excitement and hustle and bustle, that you don't lose sight of the whole point of the wedding – its deeper meaning and the central reason for its entire existence. Your gown.

— *Dave Barry*

According to *Modern Bride* magazine, the average bride spends 150 hours planning her wedding. The average groom spends 150 hours going, "Yeah, sounds good."

— *Jay Leno*

Most daughters marry men just like their fathers. Maybe that's why so many mothers cry at their weddings.

— *Bruce Wilkinson*

All I remember about my wedding day in 1967 is that the Cubs lost a double-header.

— *George Will*

Weight

The funny thing about these uniforms is that you hang them in a closet and they get smaller and smaller.

— Curt Flood, before a 1989 Old-Timers game

The chief excitement of a woman's life consists of spotting women who are fatter than she is.

— Helen Rowland

A waste is a terrible thing to mind.

— Albert Sonnenfeld

Whispering

How come when people are whispering, the only thing you can hear is your name?

— Tom Wilson

Windows

Preudhomme's Law of Window Cleaning: It's on the other side.

— Winston Preudhomme

Winning

No one ever says, "It's only a game," when their team is winning.

— Ed O'Brien

Wisdom

This morning I woke up to a cold, miserable, rainy day. So I prayed for the strength to get up, get dressed and run five miles. Then I rolled over and went back to sleep. I had prayed for strength, but received wisdom instead.

— Anonymous

Knowledge is knowing a tomato is a fruit; wisdom is not putting it in a fruit salad.

— Anonymous

If you want people to think you're wise, just agree with them.

— Leo Rosten

Great Funny Quotes

Wives

Funny how a wife can spot a blonde hair at twenty yards, yet miss the garage doors.

— *Corey Ford*

Wives are people who feel they don't dance enough.

— *Groucho Marx*

Wife: A person who can ride through the most magnificent scenery in the world with her eyes glued to the speedometer.

— *Anonymous*

Women

To judge from the covers of countless women's magazines, the two topics most interesting to women are 1) why men are all disgusting pigs and 2) how to attract men.

— *Dave Barry*

Women don't want to hear what you think. Women want to hear what they think, in a deeper voice.

— *Bill Cosby*

One of the great mysteries to me is the fact that a woman could pour hot wax on her legs, rip the hair out by the roots and still be afraid of a spider.

— *Jerry Seinfeld*

If you think women are the weaker sex, try pulling the blankets back to your side.

— *Stuart Turner*

Wood

Wood burns faster when you cut and chopped it yourself.

— *Harrison Ford*

Words

Certain tribes in Borneo do have a word for no and consequently turn down requests by nodding their heads and saying, "I'll get back to you."

— *Woody Allen*

Look in my pants pocket and give him five bucks.
   — *Yogi Berra, when he was having his blinds repaired and his son called out, "Dad, the guy is here for the Venetian blinds."*

An English professor at Vassar was impressing upon his freshman class the advantages of acquiring a large vocabulary. "Say a word out loud to yourself five times," he advised, "and it will be yours for life." A freshman in the front row closed her eyes and breathed ecstatically, "Walter, Walter, Walter, Walter, Walter . . ."
   — *Bennett Cerf*

Never use a long word when a diminutive one will do.
   — *William Safire*

Whom is a word invented to make everyone sound like a butler.
   — *Calvin Trillin*

Work
I thought at one point I could see the light at the end of the tunnel – turned out to be someone with a flashlight bringing me more work.
   — *Anonymous*

Hard work never killed anybody, but it sure has scared a lot of folks to death.
   — *Anonymous*

God put me on earth to accomplish a certain number of things. Right now I am so far behind I will never die.
   — *Anonymous*

If work was so good the rich would keep more of it for themselves.
   — *Anonymous*

Things are looking up . . . I'm now only two weeks behind.
   — *Anonymous*

Anyone can do any amount of work, provided it isn't the work he is supposed to be doing at the moment.
   — *Robert Benchley*

The volume of paper expands to fill the available briefcases.

— *Edmund Brown*

"How long have you been working here?"
    "Since the boss threatened to fire me."

— *Shelby Friedman*

The brain is a wonderful organ; it starts working the moment you get up in the morning and doesn't stop until you get into the office.

— *Robert Frost*

By working faithfully eight hours a day you may eventually get to be boss and work twelve hours a day.

— *Robert Frost*

Most people like hard work, particularly when they're paying for it.

— *Franklin Jones*

Work expands so as to fill the time available for its completion.

— *Cyril Parkinson*

Nothing reminds a woman of all that needs to be done around the house like a husband who is taking it easy.

— *Bob Phillips*

If you don't believe in the resurrection of the dead, look at any office at quitting time.

— *Robert Townsend*

By the time I was five I was out in the fields. I thought hard work was just how life was. I was 21 years old before I knew Manual Labor wasn't a Mexican.

— *Lee Trevino*

Workaholics

You know you're a workaholic when you're making a phone call from home, you hit 9 to get out.

— *Dennis Miller*

Worry

I've joined the new Don't Worry Club,
    And now I hold my breath
    I'm so afraid I'll worry
    That I'm worried half to death.

— R. Lofton Hudson

Writing

Conclusion: The place where you get tired of thinking.

— Anonymous

"I enjoyed your book immensely. Who wrote it for you?"
    "I'm so glad you liked it. Who read it to you?"

— Anonymous

The cure for writer's cramp is writer's block.

— Inigo DeLeon

Writing is easy. All you do is stare at a blank sheet of paper until drops of blood form on your forehead.

— Gene Fowler

Dr. Donne's verses are like the peace of God; they pass all understanding.

— James I

Your manuscript is both good and original; but the part that is good is not original, and the part that is original is not good.

— Samuel Johnson

Writing is not hard. Just get paper and pencil, sit down, and write it as it occurs to you. The writing is easy – it's the occurring that's hard.

— Stephen Leacock

No author dislikes to be edited as much as he dislikes not to be published.

— Russell Lynes

They say writing the first line of a book is the hardest part. Thank God that's over.

— Willie Nelson, beginning of his book

I can't write five words but that I change seven.

— *Dorothy Parker*

Yard Work

I was watching a baseball game on TV and my wife said, "Speaking of high and outside, the grass needs mowing."

— *Anonymous*

A good way to get a boy to cut the grass is to forbid him to touch the lawn mower.

— *Anonymous*

Thank goodness for the scientist who said dead leaves help a lawn in the fall.

— *Anonymous*

It was one of those perfect summer days – the sun was shining, a breeze was blowing, the birds were singing and the lawnmower was broken.

— *James Dent*

A yard is never too small for the grass to be cut with a sit-down tractor mower.

— *Kevin Nealon, on what his father taught him*

Any child who is anxious to mow the lawn is too young to do it.

— *Bob Phillips*

Yes-Men

I don't want any yes-men around me. I want everybody to tell me the truth even if it costs them their jobs.

— *Samuel Goldwyn*

Youth

I am not young enough to know everything.

— *Sir James Barrie*

Youth is such a wonderful thing. What a crime to waste it on children.

— *George Bernard Shaw*

Zeal

Zeal: A certain nervous disorder afflicting the young and inexperienced.

— *Anonymous*

About the Author

David Young is a policy advisor to the governor of Texas. He received his Bachelor of Science in Business Administration degree, Summa Cum Laude, from the University of Arkansas and his Master of Business Administration degree from The University of Texas at Austin.

David grew up in Fort Smith, Arkansas. Both of his grandfathers were born before the Civil War. He and his wife, Christina, live in Round Rock, Texas. David has traveled extensively throughout the United States, Canada and Europe, and has visited South America, Asia and the Middle East.

Also by David Young

Breakthrough Power

Breakthrough Power for Mothers

Breakthrough Power for Fathers

Breakthrough Power for Christians

Breakthrough Power for Leaders

Breakthrough Power for Athletes

Breakthrough Power for Golfers

Rebound Strong

.

www.ingramcontent.com/pod-product-compliance
Lightning Source LLC
LaVergne TN
LVHW011322080426
835513LV00006B/162